A GUIDED
TOUR OF THE
BIBLE

A GUIDED
TOUR OF THE
BIBLE

A ONE-YEAR JOURNEY
THROUGH 365 KEY
CHAPTERS OF THE BIBLE

KENNETH AND KAREN
BOA

Authentic

ATLANTA · LONDON · HYDERABAD

Authentic Publishing
We welcome your questions and comments.

USA   PO Box 444, 285 Lynnwood Ave, Tyrone, GA, 30290
      www.authenticbooks.com
UK   9 Holdom Avenue, Bletchley, Milton Keynes, Bucks, MK1 1QR
      www.authenticmedia.co.uk
India Logos Bhavan, Medchal Road, Jeedimetla Village, Secunderabad
      500 055, A.P.

A Guided Tour of the Bible
ISBN-13: 978-1-932805-92-5
ISBN-10: 1-932805-92-3

10 09 08 07 / 6 5 4 3 2 1

Published in 2007 by Authentic

Library of Congress Cataloging-in-Publication Data available

Cover design: Paul Lewis
Interior design: Angela Lewis
Editorial team: Betsy Weinrich, Megan Kassebaum

Printed in the United States of America

INTRODUCTION

The Purpose of this Book

Many people would love to know the Bible and to understand the beauty and flow of its literary narratives and interwoven themes. But because of its sheer size and structural complexity, the effort to grasp the message of the Bible seems too daunting a task. Often when people decide to join the tiny minority of people who have actually read the Scriptures from Genesis to Revelation, they get bogged down by the time they reach the books of Leviticus or Deuteronomy. The few who press on through the historical books wonder what happened to the story line when they arrive at the poets and prophets. With the multiple historical references to people, places, and events and the intricacies of the narratives, it is little wonder that people have difficulty putting the pieces of the puzzle together in a meaningful way.

With these problems in mind, we designed this handbook to guide you through the highlights of Scripture by taking you on a tour of 365 key chapters during the course of a year. By reading the introductory material for each chapter, you will get a concise overview of the Scripture reading for that day, and this will aid you in your understanding. These daily introductions present the necessary historical backgrounds, literary flow, story line, and central issues in the chapters you will read. We selected these chapters to give you the big picture of the Bible so that by the time you have completed this tour, you will have a clear grasp of the message of Scripture.

How to Use this Book

As you can quickly see by looking at any of the 365 readings, each day has four elements: one or two brief introductory paragraphs, an invitation to read the appropriate chapter from your Bible, a prayer of application that relates to the message of the chapter, and one or more meditation verses from that day's reading. Take your time as you read the introductory material so that it will become an aid to your understanding. For your chapter reading, use a translation of the Bible that is clear and accessible to you, or try more than one translation. (We used the Updated Edition of the New American Standard Bible for the direct Scripture quotations in this book.) Keep this book open during your Scripture reading so that you can refer at any time to the introductory comments.

After your Bible reading, be sure to read the prayer slowly and thoughtfully, and then take some time to personalize it and adapt it as your own response to the Scripture chapter you have just read. Finally, read the meditation passage for the day, and if there is more than one meditation verse in the chapter, you may want to select the passage that speaks most directly to you. Simply take a few moments to move slowly through the passage and reflect on each of the phrases and images. Consider writing this passage on an index card to carry with you throughout the day. In this way, you can review your passage by looking at the card at any time (e.g., waiting in line or at traffic lights). It is much better to meditate on truth than to meditate on negative thoughts about people or problems.

This book of the law shall not depart from your mouth, but you shall meditate on it day and night, so that you may be careful to do according to all that is written in it; for then you will make your way prosperous, and then you will have success. (Joshua 1:8)

Whatever is true, whatever is honorable, whatever is right, whatever is pure, whatever is lovely, whatever is of good repute, if there is any excellence and if anything worthy of praise, dwell on these things. (Philippians 4:8)

DAY 1—GENESIS 1

G enesis, the book of beginnings, provides us with a cosmic perspective on the foundation of the heavens and the earth as well as the climax of God's creation—humans who have been created in His image and likeness. In the first three days God orders His creation, and in the last three days He populates it. Day 1 corresponds to day 4, day 2 to day 5, and day 3 to day 6. At the end of the sixth day, God was pleased with His creative work and declared it "very good."

In this chapter we discover our true dignity as people who have been created by and for God as His image-bearers, and we see the extensive authority with which He entrusted us.

READING OF GENESIS 1

Prayer:

Lord, I am amazed at the diversity, beauty, and complexity of Your creation. Heaven and earth are full of the majesty of Your glory, and the created order points beyond itself to You. Give me a greater sense of wonder and awe at all that You have done, and do not let me take Your wonderful world for granted.

MEDITATION PASSAGE FOR TODAY:

verse 27

The climax of Genesis 1 was the creation of the man and the woman, and the climax of Genesis 2 was the covenant relationship between the man and the woman. Today's chapter is crucial to our understanding of human nature: God did not create us the way we are now, but we changed ourselves through the tragedy of the fall. The fundamental issue in the temptation scene was trusting God enough to believe that He has our best interests at heart. When the man and the woman decided that they had a better idea than God of what their best interests looked like, they turned from saying "Thy will be done" to "My will be done." Thus they were spiritually separated from God, and their character and destiny were radically changed.

READING OF GENESIS 3

Prayer:

Lord, I realize that I have participated in this scene of rebellion against You, and like Adam and Eve, I have sought to experience life on my terms. By Your grace, I acknowledge this sin of pride and ask You to root out of me all that is contrary to Your purposes and character so that Christ may be all in all in my life.

MEDITATION PASSAGE FOR TODAY:

verse 15

DAY 3—GENESIS 4

The fall in Genesis 3 immediately had ripple effects. Rebellion against God's good and loving purposes distorted our relationships with God, with ourselves, with others, and with the created order. The barrier with God changed us and produced internal and external conflicts; the murder of Abel by his brother Cain is a prototype of the hostility and social degeneration caused by the pride and selfishness of sin. Although the line of godly Abel was cut off, God replaced him with Seth and his descendants. It would be through this godly line that the ancestors of the Messiah would spring forth.

READING OF GENESIS 4

Prayer:

Lord, I thank You that Your Word reveals not only the depth of human sin and iniquity, but also the height of Your love and gracious purposes. Help me remember that sin and disobedience are always destructive, and that righteousness and obedience to You are always creative and life-giving.

MEDITATION PASSAGE FOR TODAY:

verses 25-26

Day 4—Genesis 6

The longevity of human life prior to the flood turned out to be a curse that only increased human malevolence and wickedness. Because of the rampant spread of evil, God took radical measures to destroy the ungodly in order to preserve a tiny remnant of the godly. It was only in Noah and his family that righteousness was to be found, and the Lord instructed Noah to prepare for the universal destruction that He would bring upon the earth. In this way, a remnant of humanity and of animal life would be preserved through the violent waters of the flood.

READING OF GENESIS 6

Prayer:

Lord, I am astonished by the level of human wickedness that You endured until the day of destruction finally removed this plague from the earth. I am also amazed at Your patience in my life, and I ask that by Your grace, I would not allow sin and rebellion to fester and multiply in my thoughts, words, and deeds. Thank You for Your forgiveness and cleansing.

MEDITATION PASSAGE FOR TODAY:

verses 5-7

DAY 5—GENESIS 7

B ecause Noah found grace in the eyes of the Lord, God instructed him in how to build a stable ark that would withstand the flood waters for a year and preserve him and his family through this devastating judgment. Noah put his faith into practice and obediently fulfilled God's instructions, though it cost him and his sons decades of toil and ridicule. Noah also obeyed God's mandate to populate the ark with two each of unclean animals and seven each of clean animals and birds.

READING OF GENESIS 7

Prayer:

Lord, I am grateful for this account of Your obedient servant Noah who trusted You enough to honor You and obey You even when Your instructions didn't seem to make sense. Thank You for the way this great ark typifies the grace of Christ who delivered us from the flood of sin and death.

MEDITATION PASSAGE FOR TODAY:

verses 5, 23

DAY 6—GENESIS 8

With the receding of the flood waters, Noah opened the window of the ark and sent out a raven and a dove. The third time he sent out the dove, the bird settled down and did not return. When the earth was dried, Noah obeyed God's instructions to go out of the ark and to repopulate the earth with the animals and with his own descendants. In response to Noah's burnt offerings on the altar he built, the Lord promised that He would never again destroy the earth through another catastrophic deluge. Instead, the earth would enjoy its annual seasons as long as it remains.

READING OF GENESIS 8

Prayer:

Lord, I am grateful for Your servant Noah and his faithfulness to Your commandments. As a result, all of us are descended from Adam through Noah, a righteous man in his time. May I likewise exhibit Your righteousness in my generation.

MEDITATION PASSAGE FOR TODAY:

verses 17, 22

DAY 7—GENESIS 9

After the flood, the Lord reinstated His mandate for humanity to "Be fruitful and multiply, and fill the earth." He also gave Noah and his descendants animal as well as plant life to eat, but He stipulated that flesh could not be consumed with its lifeblood.

God also established a covenant with Noah and his descendants and gave him the rainbow as the sign of this covenant. It appears that ecological conditions on earth were radically different after the flood. It may be that more rapid fermentation of grape juice was one of these differences (this would account for the drunkenness of Noah).

READING OF GENESIS 9

Prayer:

Lord, I thank You for Your covenant relationship with Noah, and for this account of Your faithfulness to him and his descendants. I am grateful that You made me in Your image and that You have created me for a purpose.

MEDITATION PASSAGE FOR TODAY:

verses 6-7

DAY 8—GENESIS 11

I t is remarkable that prior to the construction of the tower of Babel, there was one universal language. In violation of God's command to multiply and populate the earth, the people sought to stay in one place rather than be "scattered abroad over the face of the whole earth." By confusing their language, the Lord forced the people to obey His mandate and thwarted their arrogant attempt to attain greatness on their terms. With the sudden multiplicity of languages, the people were forced to populate other parts of the earth.

This chapter includes a genealogical line that traces the descendants of Shem to Abram, the key figure of the next portion of Genesis.

READING OF GENESIS 11

Prayer:

Lord, Your wisdom and power are great, and Your purposes stand to all generations. I am grateful that You are so sovereign that the plans of those who rebel against You actually contribute to Your plan and that Your Word gives us a long-term perspective on human history.

MEDITATION PASSAGE FOR TODAY:

verse 9

This crucial chapter records the calling of Abram out of all the people of the earth and the threefold outline of the Abrahamic covenant: land, seed, and blessing. God's promise to give Abram and his descendants a land and a permanent lineage is the theme of much of the Old Testament, and this covenant also affirms that in Abram, "all the families of the earth will be blessed." The name of Abraham has indeed become great, and he is now revered by Jews, Muslims, and Christians.

Abram was a man of faith who learned to recognize the voice of God, to call upon His name, and to obey Him.

READING OF GENESIS 12

Prayer:

Lord, I thank You for the faith of this man who was willing to trust You and to risk everything on Your promises and commands. I am also grateful that in spite of his lapses and shortcomings, You continued to use him, just as You desire to do with me.

MEDITATION PASSAGE FOR TODAY:

verses 1–3

G enesis 15 is crucial to an understanding of Abram's relationship with the Lord who called him out of Ur of the Chaldeans to be the father of nations. When the Lord promised that his descendants would be like the stars in number, Abram "believed in the Lord; and He reckoned it to him as righteousness." The Lord then ratified His blood covenant with His servant and his descendants by passing between the pieces of the animals. Because Abram believed God, he was justified by grace through faith.

READING OF GENESIS 15

Prayer:

Lord, Your faithfulness and loyal love reach to the heavens, and none of Your good promises ever fail. I ask for the grace to trust You more and to believe Your promises.

MEDITATION PASSAGE FOR TODAY:

verses 1, 5–6

DAY 11—GENESIS 18

When three men appeared to Abraham, they affirmed that in spite of the old age of Abraham and Sarah, they would be the parents of the son of the covenant promise that God had made earlier. When Sarah laughed within herself, the Lord responded, "Is anything too difficult for the Lord?"

One of the three men was the angel of the Lord, evidently a manifestation of the preincarnate Christ, since He is called the Lord. Abraham, concerned with the righteousness and justice of God, intercedes on behalf of the people of Sodom until the Lord agrees that if there are only ten righteous people there, He will not destroy the city.

READING OF GENESIS 18

Prayer:

Lord, I thank You that nothing is too difficult for You. I am also grateful that Your character is perfect and that Your ways are just, righteous, and true. Let me trust in Your ways and walk in them.

MEDITATION PASSAGE FOR TODAY:

verses 14, 19, 25

DAY 12—GENESIS 21

J ust as He had predicted, the Lord visited Sarah and brought about the miracle of the birth of Isaac, the covenant son He had promised to Abraham and Sarah. This time, Sarah laughed with joy and said, "Who would have said to Abraham that Sarah would nurse children? Yet I have borne him a son in his old age."

As Isaac grew, tension also grew between Sarah and Hagar until Hagar was sent out into the wilderness. The Lord provided for her and Ishmael and preserved their lives. Meanwhile, Abraham continued to grow in faith and called on the name of the Lord, the Everlasting God.

READING OF GENESIS 21

Prayer:

Lord, like Abraham and Sarah, I often try to take matters into my own hands and seek to accomplish things in my own timing, way, and power. I thank You that Your ways are far above my own, and I ask for the grace to trust in Your ways without trying to manipulate the outcome.

MEDITATION PASSAGE FOR TODAY:

verses 5–7, 33

DAY 13—GENESIS 22

O ver the years of walking with the Lord, Abraham learned to trust God's voice and obey it. As his faith grew, the Lord increased the level of risk, and the supreme test recorded in this chapter revealed on the outside what God had been working for years on the inside. For Abraham to sacrifice Isaac, the son of the covenant through whom Abraham's descendants would be named, it would mean that the only way the promises could be fulfilled would be for Isaac to rise from the dead (Hebrews 11:19). God was pleased with Abraham's demonstration and honored his faith by providing a substitute for his son.

READING OF GENESIS 22

Prayer:

Lord, I am stunned at the level of trust and obedience Your servant Abraham exhibited in his willingness to risk everything on Your command. I ask that I would learn to trust You more and more and let loose of the things that would compete with my allegiance to You.

MEDITATION PASSAGE FOR TODAY:

verses 12, 16–18

Abraham's careful instructions to his servant reveal the concern he had in finding God's intended bride for his special son Isaac. He knew that he and his family had been called by the Lord to be a representative people through whom all the families of the earth would be blessed, and he did not want disobedience or expedience to corrupt this godly line of destiny. Rebekah for her part discerned that more was involved in this than an ordinary arranged marriage, and she took a risk in going with Abraham's servant to meet his son Isaac.

READING OF GENESIS 24

Prayer:

Lord, the Scriptures affirm that when people are willing to obey You by walking out into the unknown and trusting in Your guidance, You always honor their faith. Let me maintain the proper object of faith by fixing my eyes on Jesus and pursuing Him with a whole heart.

MEDITATION PASSAGE FOR TODAY:

verses 40, 48

E sau had already sold his birthright to his conniving brother Jacob for a bowl of red stew, and now the supplanter deceived his father Isaac to obtain Esau's blessing as well. Rebekah encouraged her favorite son to do this, thinking that in this way, God's promise that "the older shall serve the younger" (Genesis 25:23) would be fulfilled. The plot worked, but not in the way they thought. Jacob succeeded in gaining his brother's blessing, but he had to flee for his life and live for decades away from his country. In addition, Rebekah experienced the unexpected sorrow of never seeing her son Jacob again.

READING OF GENESIS 27

Prayer:

Lord, Your Word reveals the consequences of taking matters into our own hands, even when it involves our attempts to fulfill Your promises. Please guard my steps from manipulating people and circumstances to obtain my idea of what You want rather than submitting to Your plan that is always better than my own.

MEDITATION PASSAGE FOR TODAY:

verse 29

After being sent away with the blessing of his father Isaac, Jacob went to his father's family in Haran where he was to find his wife. It is ironic that this deceiver would be outfoxed by an even more consummate deceiver, his uncle Laban.

On his way to Haran, Jacob encountered the presence of God in his dream about a ladder that reached to heaven, and the Lord affirmed His covenant with him as He had done with Abraham and Isaac before him. The Lord promised to be with him and to preserve and protect him in all his undertakings, and Jacob realized that the place of his encounter with God was a special place, the house of God (Bethel).

READING OF GENESIS 28

Prayer:

Lord, how awesome is the Son of Man upon whom the angels of God ascend and descend! You keep Your covenant and are personally involved in the affairs of Your people. Let me walk with You, and keep me in Your way.

MEDITATION PASSAGE FOR TODAY:

verses 12–16

I t was painfully obvious that Joseph was his father Jacob's favorite son. When Joseph (perhaps unwisely) shared his dreams with his brothers, they hated him even more, because it appeared that he had ambitions of ruling over them. When the brothers saw an opportunity to get rid of Joseph, their jealousy prompted them to sell him into slavery in Egypt, presumably never to be seen again. The conspirators lied to their father Jacob and claimed that Joseph had been killed by a wild beast. At first glance, it would appear that Joseph's dreams could never be fulfilled.

READING OF GENESIS 37

Prayer:

Lord, You are the sovereign God who orchestrates human circumstances according to a wisdom that transcends our understanding. May I learn to trust in Your plans and purposes for my life, especially in times when the outcome seems doubtful.

MEDITATION PASSAGE FOR TODAY:

verses 9–11

DAY 18—GENESIS 39

I n spite of Joseph's ups and downs, it is clear from this account that the Lord was with him and would not abandon him. Joseph found favor in Potiphar's sight, and the Egyptian's household prospered under Joseph's prudent management. Potiphar's implicit trust in Joseph suddenly came to an end when his wife accused Joseph of attempted rape after Joseph refused her enticing offers. Thus, Joseph was rewarded with prison for his actual fidelity and moral character. Even there, however, the hand of the Lord remained upon him as he was being prepared for God's good purposes.

READING OF GENESIS 39

Prayer:

Lord, when I consider Joseph's difficulties, it is easy to see how he could have despaired and wondered if the dreams You gave him would ever be fulfilled. Give me the grace to cling to Your character in times when my circumstances seem hopeless and pointless.

MEDITATION PASSAGE FOR TODAY:

verses 2–3, 21

D uring his years of imprisonment, the Lord continued to nurture and prepare Joseph for a destiny so significant that Joseph would not have believed it even if he were told on a solemn oath.

Joseph was not only a capable and prudent man, but he was also given the divine gift of being able to interpret dreams. When he correctly interpreted the dreams of Pharaoh's chief butler and chief baker, Joseph hoped that the butler would mention him to Pharaoh so that he would be extricated from the dungeon. Instead, he continued to languish in prison.

READING OF GENESIS 40

Prayer:

Lord, it is easy to read this account with complete hindsight and realize that everything You allowed in Joseph's life worked together for his ultimate good. But Joseph did not have this hindsight and could only see things as they were happening. Grant me the wisdom to see things more from Your perspective and to view my temporal circumstances in light of Your eternal purposes.

MEDITATION PASSAGE FOR TODAY:

verse 8

T wo years after the incident with the butler and baker, the Lord troubled Pharaoh with a disturbing dream that cried out for an interpretation. It was then that the butler recalled Joseph's ability to interpret dreams and informed Pharaoh about him. When Pharaoh summoned Joseph, the Hebrew's fortunes changed suddenly and dramatically. Not only was he granted the ability to interpret Pharaoh's dreams, but he also was given the wisdom to know how to act in the most effective way to avert the disastrous consequences of the coming famine in Egypt. In the course of only a few hours, Joseph was elevated from imprisonment to the position of prime minister in Egypt.

READING OF GENESIS 41

Prayer:

Lord, You are able to bring a person or a nation down in a day and to raise them up suddenly at Your good pleasure. All things are in Your hands, and I want to learn to take this to heart when I find myself discouraged and disheartened.

MEDITATION PASSAGE FOR TODAY:

verses 16, 25, 28

DAY 21—GENESIS 42

The Lord used the great famine to orchestrate an encounter between Joseph and his brothers. When his brothers came and bowed down before him, Joseph remembered the dreams he had experienced years before and realized they were finally being fulfilled. Joseph tested his brothers to see what was in their hearts, and they did not realize who he was or that he could understand their language. He required them to leave Simeon in Egypt while they returned to Canaan to bring their youngest brother to confirm their words.

READING OF GENESIS 42

Prayer:

Lord, I thank You for this very real account of the gradual process of reconciliation of estranged relationships. May I examine my own relationships and humble myself enough to seek out reconciliation and closure with anyone I have injured in the past.

MEDITATION PASSAGE FOR TODAY:

verse 22

J acob resisted sending his sons back to Egypt even though he knew that Simeon had been detained there. He tried to avert action because he did not want to lose Benjamin, but the severity of the famine forced his hand. At this point, Judah assured him that he would be responsible for Benjamin's welfare.

Once again Joseph's brothers prostrated themselves before him in fulfillment of the dreams he had been given. It was an emotional moment for Joseph to see his full brother Benjamin, and he sought to control himself during the serving of the meal.

READING OF GENESIS 43

Prayer:

Lord, I see how Your purposeful hand intervenes in human affairs and how Your plans are not thwarted by our disobedience and manipulation. Grant that I may rest in Your care and entrust my affairs to You in all things.

MEDITATION PASSAGE FOR TODAY:

verse 14

DAY 23—GENESIS 44

O nce again Joseph tested the hearts of his brothers to see how they would respond when he would make a claim on Benjamin to be his slave. His brother Judah made good on his promise to Jacob to become surety for Benjamin; when Joseph saw Judah's willingness to sacrifice himself to save Jacob from the grief of losing Benjamin, Joseph was ready to reveal himself to his brothers. Thus Joseph was able to witness the repentance and remorse of his brothers for the injury they had committed years earlier to him.

READING OF GENESIS 44

Prayer:

Lord, Your servant Joseph dealt wisely with his brothers, and I thank You for this powerful account of gradual character development. Help me remember that injuring others always has long-term consequences, and teach me to treat others with mercy and grace.

MEDITATION PASSAGE FOR TODAY:

verse 16

DAY 24—GENESIS 45

This chapter completes the process of reconciliation between Joseph and his brothers and reveals the need for the grace of forgiveness in order to restore estranged relationships. When Joseph revealed his true identity to his brothers, he also communicated the divine purpose behind the pains he experienced over the years: "Now do not be grieved or angry with yourselves, because you sold me here, for God sent me before you to preserve life." Thus, Joseph was reunited with his brothers, and the children of Israel were brought into Egypt to prevent them from losing their identity through intermarriage with the Canaanites.

READING OF GENESIS 45

Prayer:

Lord, I marvel at the graciousness of Your servant Joseph and at his willingness to extend forgiveness and grace to his brothers. Give me the wisdom to see things from Your perspective so that I will not suppose that people injure me in ways that cannot be redeemed by Your higher purposes.

MEDITATION PASSAGE FOR TODAY:

verses 5, 7–8

A t the end of Jacob's sojourn in Egypt, he blessed his sons in accordance with their character and the future of their tribes. Joseph made elaborate arrangements for Jacob's embalming and burial, and a large retinue of Egyptian officials accompanied them for the solemn burial and lamentation in Canaan. Sadly, Joseph's brothers assumed that their father Jacob was the restraining influence that kept Joseph from seeking vengeance on them for their sin against him. When they approached him after Jacob's death, Joseph had to assure them that although they meant evil against him, "God meant it for good in order to bring about this present result, to preserve many people alive."

READING OF GENESIS 50

Prayer:

Lord, I thank You for Joseph's words of comfort, wisdom, and perspective to his brothers. Apart from a divine perspective, I realize that I would be vulnerable to bitterness, resentment, and wrath when people intend evil against me.

MEDITATION PASSAGE FOR TODAY:

verses 19–20

DAY 26—EXODUS 1

I n the four centuries that transpired between Genesis 50 and Exodus 1, the condition of the children of Israel degenerated from one of privilege and protection to one of prejudice and bondage. The descendants of Jacob multiplied so rapidly that they became a threat to the Egyptians, who reacted by plotting to exterminate their male children. The oppression reached such a pitch that the people of Israel lost all hope because of their forced labor and complete insecurity.

READING OF EXODUS 1

Prayer:

Lord, I realize that You often have to bring us to the end of ourselves before we will acknowledge our desperate condition and call upon You for deliverance. May I learn to respond quickly to You rather than resist You through my stubborn pride and autonomy.

MEDITATION PASSAGE FOR TODAY:

verses 8, 12

DAY 27—EXODUS 2

I n this chapter, the scene shifts from the children of Israel as a whole to a specific family God would use to provide deliverance for His people in response to their cry for help. The Lord sovereignly guided the process so that Pharaoh's daughter would raise a Hebrew child that otherwise was destined for death. She even hired Moses' mother to nurse him, and thus Moses was aware of his true identity with the people of God.

When Moses sought to deliver his people on his own timing and terms, he failed and had to flee for his life to the land of Midian. While he was there, his people back in Egypt remembered the God of their fathers and cried out to Him to deliver them from bondage.

READING OF EXODUS 2

Prayer:

Lord, I see how You prepare to save Your people even before they call upon Your name. I thank You that You are concerned with the things that concern me, and that You always desire what is best for me.

MEDITATION PASSAGE FOR TODAY:

verses 10, 23–25

Only after an additional forty years of personal preparation in the wilderness of Midian was Moses ready to become the leader and deliverer the Lord was grooming him to be. His personal encounter with the presence of the living God at the burning bush permanently transformed him and gave him a desire to seek the Lord for the remainder of his days. The great I AM commissioned Moses to represent the children of Israel before Pharaoh and to perform signs and wonders until Pharaoh would finally let the people go.

READING OF EXODUS 3

Prayer:

Lord, You are the God of Abraham, the God of Isaac, and the God of Jacob, the everlasting I AM WHO I AM. I thank You that You stoop to show compassion for Your people and deliver them from their servitude to sin and death.

MEDITATION PASSAGE FOR TODAY:

verses 6, 14–15

M oses repeatedly objected to becoming God's chosen in-
strument of deliverance for his people, and the Lord
answered each of his excuses. Moses' fifth objection to send
someone else angered the Lord because of the lack of faith it
represented. Even here, the Lord made provision for a spokes-
man to the people, and Aaron was already on his way to visit
his brother Moses. When Moses and Aaron returned to Egypt,
the Lord gave them favor with the children of Israel who realized that the Lord had finally visited them and looked on their
affliction.

READING OF EXODUS 4

Prayer:

*Lord, You meet Your people at their point of need and authen-
ticate Yourself in so many ways. I thank You that You prepare
creative ways of delivering us from the servitude and monotony
of sin, and that You invite us to participate in Your works and
ways.*

MEDITATION PASSAGE FOR TODAY:

verses 5, 11, 31

A s the Lord had predicted, Pharaoh rejected Moses' request and denied the Lord ("Who is the LORD that I should obey His voice to let Israel go?"). As a result, matters turned even worse for the children of Israel, since Pharaoh, accusing them of being lazy, now mandated that they must gather their own straw without reducing the daily quota of bricks. This naturally made Moses odious in his own people's sight; far from delivering them from their bondage, he had actually increased it. It is therefore not surprising that Moses complained to the Lord and wanted to resign his divine commission.

READING OF EXODUS 5

Prayer:

Lord, I know that when You show Your people a new thing, You test them to see what is in their hearts. Teach me to look to You alone as my source of provision in all things, and not to put my hope in people, possessions, or circumstances to deliver me.

MEDITATION PASSAGE FOR TODAY:

verses 22–23

Day 31—Exodus 6

I t often seems that the Lord does not work until we reach the end of our own resources. Now that all seemed lost, God assured Moses that He was about to guide His people out of Egypt with an outstretched arm and with great judgments. Hearing these words of assurance, Moses relayed them to his people, but in their anguish of spirit they would not heed him. Nevertheless, the Lord re-commissioned Moses for the great task he was to undertake.

READING OF EXODUS 6

Prayer:

Lord, I thank You that You revealed Yourself to Your people as Yahweh, the personal, covenant-keeping God who was, and is, and is to come, the Almighty. Thank You for your concern for our plight and our needs. May I always be responsive to Your gracious initiatives.

MEDITATION PASSAGE FOR TODAY:

verses 2–8

B ecause of his negative experience with Pharaoh and his people, Moses needed reassurance from the Lord about His plan and purposes for His people. Moses was called to play a significant leadership role, and he needed to learn the wisdom of leaning solely on the Lord to accomplish this daunting task.

Pharaoh's magicians were able to accomplish just enough with their enchantments that Pharaoh could rationalize the miraculous signs of Aaron's rod and the first plague of blood as being religious chicanery. Just as the Lord had predicted, Pharaoh's heart grew hard.

READING OF EXODUS 7

Prayer:

Lord, You have complete authority over heaven and earth, and nothing is too difficult for You. When I review Your mighty acts in history, it increases my confidence that You can work powerfully in my own life as well.

MEDITATION PASSAGE FOR TODAY:

verses 4–5

DAY 33—EXODUS 8

The next three plagues of frogs, lice, and flies added to Egypt's woes but failed to convince Pharaoh to let the children of Israel go. Once again, the magicians were able to create a paltry imitation of the plague of frogs, and once again, Pharaoh hardened his heart when the plague abated. With the plague of lice, however, the magicians themselves recognized that this was the finger of God and no enchantment. Nevertheless, Pharaoh refused to heed them just as he did after the plague of flies was removed in accordance with Moses' promise.

READING OF EXODUS 8

Prayer:

Lord, I realize that there appears to be no limit to the human propensity to deny and rationalize the truth even when it is staring us in the face. May I not harden my heart and resist the things You wish to teach me, but may I be supple and sensitive to Your desires.

MEDITATION PASSAGE FOR TODAY:

verses 10, 19

As the plagues upon Egypt progress, it becomes increasingly obvious that they are highly selective — none of them reaches or affects the children of Israel in their dwellings in the land of Goshen. The mounting pressure upon Pharaoh is evident in his growing concessions to Moses, but he still refuses to comply with Moses' full demands. After the pestilence on Egypt's livestock and the plague of boils, the hardness of Pharaoh's heart led to yet another prediction of a new plague. The plague of severe hail was so devastating that it appeared that Pharaoh would relent. But as Moses told him, "I know that you do not yet fear the LORD God."

READING OF EXODUS 9

Prayer:

Lord, the ability of people to resist and rebel against You is so great that it is frightening. Give me the wisdom to fear Your word and respond to the things You proclaim and exhort.

MEDITATION PASSAGE FOR TODAY:

verses 12, 14

T he pattern of the plagues shows a gradual increase in intensity and severity as they progress. As they grow more devastating, Pharaoh's own servants urgently exhort him to relent and accede to Moses' repeated request ("Do you not realize that Egypt is destroyed?"). But Pharaoh wanted to determine the terms of departure, and the destructive plague of locusts that came upon Egypt brought him to the point of acknowledging his sin but not to the point of letting them go. The ninth plague carried a palpable darkness to the land followed by a final hardening of Pharaoh's heart.

READING OF EXODUS 10

Prayer:

Lord, no one is able to stand against You, though we often try to resist Your purposes. Help me remember the fleeting and limited nature of human power and wealth in contrast to the permanent and infinite nature of Your power and greatness.

MEDITATION PASSAGE FOR TODAY:

verses 20, 27

I n spite of nine awful plagues that decimated the land of Egypt but did not touch the children of Israel, Pharaoh stubbornly refused to permit the people to depart; in his pride, he was allowing his own nation to be devastated. This time, however, the Lord told Moses about the coming tenth plague, the worst one of all. With the loss of every firstborn in the land of Egypt, including Pharaoh's own firstborn child, Pharaoh would finally relent. By this time, Moses had attained greatness in the sight of the Egyptians as well as his own people. Before they left Egypt, the people would finally receive their "wages" for their years of servitude by receiving articles of silver and gold from the Egyptians.

READING OF EXODUS 11

Prayer:

Lord, You accomplish Your purposes in spite of the stubbornness of those who oppose You. All life is in Your hands; You give life and You take it away, and no one can legitimately accuse You of injustice or untruth.

MEDITATION PASSAGE FOR TODAY:

verse 3

This crucial chapter institutes the Passover and outlines its meaning as a portrait of redemption through sacrificial blood. Ultimately, the Passover points beyond itself to the voluntary sacrifice of God's own Son, the Lamb of God who takes away the sin of the world. The lamb had to be in its prime, without blemish, tested for a period of days, and sacrificed between 3:00 and 6:00 in the afternoon. The blood of the lamb had to be applied to the lintel and doorposts of each house so that the angel of death would spare the firstborn.

In his grief at the loss of his own firstborn, Pharaoh finally relented and commanded the people of Israel to depart from Egypt.

READING OF EXODUS 12

Prayer:

Lord, I thank You for this detailed prefiguring of the sacrificial death of Your Son. During this awesome night You redeemed Your people and set them free from their servitude so that they could be free to serve You in love and truth.

MEDITATION PASSAGE FOR TODAY:

verses 13–14, 26–27

T he feasts of Unleavened Bread and Passover marked the beginning of Israel as a redeemed nation before God, and these feasts were instituted as an annual memorial of the Lord's mighty acts on His people's behalf. From then on, they would set apart every firstborn animal to the Lord and redeem every firstborn son before the Lord. When they set out, the Lord guided them by way of the wilderness of the Red Sea so they would not change their minds and return to Egypt. Had they gone the easier coastal way, they would have been subsequently overwhelmed by the Egyptian army.

READING OF EXODUS 13

Prayer:

Lord, You delight in deeds of deliverance and in providing life and hope for those who turn to You. May I walk in complete dependence upon You and not change my mind by seeking to return to the values and lusts of this world system.

MEDITATION PASSAGE FOR TODAY:

verses 9, 21–22

DAY 39—EXODUS 14

To their horror, the children of Israel discovered in the wilderness that Pharaoh had changed his mind and was pursuing them with his chariots and army. When they cried out in despair, Moses told them to stand still and see the salvation of the Lord. The Angel of God went behind them and the pillar of cloud became a barrier of protection between them and the Egyptian army. Throughout the night, the miracle of the parting of the waters made it possible for the children of Israel to cross the sea on dry ground, and on the next morning the Lord closed the waters on the pursuing Egyptians and overthrew them. Thus, the Lord delivered His people through blood (the Passover) and through water (the Exodus).

READING OF EXODUS 14

Prayer:

Lord, You are the God of surprises. Just when it appears that all is lost, You do a new thing and deliver Your people through creative acts. May I learn to know not only Your works, but also Your ways.

MEDITATION PASSAGE FOR TODAY:

verses 13, 31

I n the days that followed the Exodus, the Lord provided for His people and protected them in the wilderness. Now that they had been redeemed, it was necessary that they be set apart to God in a covenant relationship and instructed in His ways so that they could become a holy people. God invited them to obey His voice and keep His covenant so that they would be a special treasure to Him above all people. When the Lord manifested Himself to the children of Israel through thunder, lightening, a thick cloud, an earthquake, and the blast of a trumpet on Mount Sinai, the people were terrified.

READING OF EXODUS 19

Prayer:

Lord, You are holy and awesome. The powers of nature point beyond themselves to Your infinitely greater power and wonders. Let me remember that when I draw near to You, I am in the presence of a consuming fire.

MEDITATION PASSAGE FOR TODAY:

verses 5–6

DAY 41—EXODUS 20

T he revelation of the Ten Commandments on Mount Sinai displayed the Lord's perfection of character and His desire that His people also reflect that character in their walk with Him and with one another. The first four commandments concern our vertical relationship with God, and the last six commandments concern our horizontal relationships with the people in our lives. These commandments contain the essence of rightly ordered spiritual and social life and are not merely concerned with external actions, but also with internal attitudes. Seen this way, they are impossible to attain through human effort, and they reveal our need for the grace of God.

READING OF EXODUS 20

Prayer:

Lord, You are a community of three Persons whose perfect character is the absolute basis for the true, the beautiful, and the good. By Your grace, may I invite You to display Your character and righteousness through me.

MEDITATION PASSAGE FOR TODAY:

verses 3, 5–6

DAY 42—EXODUS 32

After the Lord revealed His judgments and ratified His blood covenant with the people, Moses went up into the mountain where he received the instructions for the tabernacle and the two tablets of the Testimony. During his forty-day absence, the people corrupted themselves and degenerated into idolatry. Moses interceded with the Lord on their behalf and disciplined them. In his love for the Lord, Moses appealed to God's reputation in the sight of the nations, and in his love for his people, Moses cried out to the Lord for their forgiveness.

READING OF EXODUS 32

Prayer:

Lord, how quickly we turn aside from walking with You, particularly when we are distracted by the cares of this world and suppose that You are distant. Let me love You enough to be concerned with the honor of Your name and to treat You as holy in the affairs of this life.

MEDITATION PASSAGE FOR TODAY:

verses 12–13

DAY 43—LEVITICUS 16

The Book of Leviticus was revealed at the foot of Mount Sinai as the Lord instructed His people in the ways of holiness. The moral, civil, and ceremonial laws were designed to provide order, stability, justice, and righteousness in the theocratic covenant community of Israel so that they would be set apart from all other nations. Those who have been redeemed must also be sanctified, and the central provision for sanctification in Israel was the sacrificial system with the priesthood and the tabernacle. The holiest day of the year was Yom Kippur, the Day of Atonement, during which the consecrated high priest would enter the Holy Place with the blood of a goat as a sin offering for the people.

READING OF LEVITICUS 16

Prayer:

Lord, no one can approach Your holiness apart from the shedding of blood for the remission of sin. I thank You that I can boldly come to Your throne of grace through the shed blood of Your righteous Son, Jesus Christ.

MEDITATION PASSAGE FOR TODAY:

verses 16, 30

B y this time, Israel had ample opportunities to grumble and complain about their conditions, their food, and their leadership. The longer they were away from Egypt, the more they idealized it and wanted to return. Numbers 13-14, however, marks a permanent change in their destiny when they drew back in disbelief at Kadesh. After sending out representatives from each of the twelve tribes to investigate the promised land, the people were disheartened by the majority report. In spite of Caleb's words of encouragement, the majority opinion prevailed.

READING OF NUMBERS 13

Prayer:

Lord, I realize that it is not my circumstances, but the perspective I bring to my circumstances that makes all the difference. Grant that I may see things from a biblical point of view rather than a worldly perspective, so that I will trust You enough to obey You.

MEDITATION PASSAGE FOR TODAY:

verse 30

C onvinced that the Lord did not have their best interests at heart, the people wanted to select a leader who would guide them back to Egypt. Joshua and Caleb urged the congregation not to rebel against the Lord but to trust Him enough to protect them as they obediently claimed the promised land. Once again, Moses had to intercede for his people before the Lord, and once again the Lord pardoned the children of Israel. Nevertheless, there were grave consequences for their failure to believe God, and the generation of the Exodus lost its opportunity to be the generation of the conquest. From that point, everyone twenty years old and above would perish in the wilderness. It would be their children who would conquer the land.

READING OF NUMBERS 14

Prayer:

Lord, it is frightening to realize that I can commit the sin of unused potential by drawing back in disbelief. I ask for the faith to honor You in spite of appearances to the contrary and to believe that You always desire what is best for me.

MEDITATION PASSAGE FOR TODAY:

verses 7–9, 18

After an additional 38 years of wilderness wandering, the new generation of Israelites needed to be prepared spiritually, morally, and physically to conquer the promised land. Near the end of his life, Moses taught the people in the plains of Moab and communicated God's ordinances, statutes, and testimonies a second time. Moses began his series of exhortations by reviewing God's dealings with His people since their time at Mount Sinai after the Exodus. He focused on the tragedy of disbelief at Kadesh and the consequences that followed.

READING OF DEUTERONOMY 1

Prayer:

Lord, I thank You that You instruct me in the way of life through Your revealed Word. May I treasure Your teachings and take them to heart so that my way will not be impeded by the sins of disbelief, autonomy, and rebellion.

MEDITATION PASSAGE FOR TODAY:

verses 21, 29–31

Moses continued his review of the works and ways of God among His people by reminding them of their encounters with the people of Edom, Moab, and Ammon. He also reminded them of their conquest of Sihon and the Amorites to provide them with a sense of perspective on the way God had gone before them, guided them, provided for them, and protected them. The clearer they grasped God's faithfulness in the past, the better they would be able to trust Him for the challenges of the present.

READING OF DEUTERONOMY 2

Prayer:

Lord, it is good for me to review Your dealings with me in the past so that I will have enough perspective to trust You actively in the present. Give me a sanctified memory and a growing sense of gratitude for what You have done in my life.

MEDITATION PASSAGE FOR TODAY:

verse 7

A fter their conquest of Sihon, the Lord gave His people victory over Og and the people of Bashan. The tribes of Reuben and Gad as well as half the tribe of Manasseh possessed the land and cities that were conquered in the Transjordan. At this point, Moses asked God to allow him to cross over and see the land beyond the Jordan before his death, but the Lord refused to do this because of Moses' disobedience when he struck the rock in anger at the grumbling of the people. Instead, the Lord allowed Moses to see the land from a distance at the top of Pisgah across from Jericho.

READING OF DEUTERONOMY 3

Prayer:

Lord, Your faithfulness and loyal love for Your people are great, in spite of the fact that they rarely appreciate what You have done for them. May I remember Your mighty deeds and acts of lovingkindness and treasure them in my heart.

MEDITATION PASSAGE FOR TODAY:

verses 22, 24

DAY 49—DEUTERONOMY 4

Moses exhorted the new generation in the plains of Moab to take heed to themselves, to remember the things they have seen, and to teach them to their children and grandchildren. He also warned them against the insidious lure of idolatry and the human tendency to worship images of our own making rather than serve the invisible God. Sadly, Moses also predicted that they would indeed succumb to idolatry and suffer the consequences of being scattered among the nations until they turn back to the Lord in their distress.

READING OF DEUTERONOMY 4

Prayer:

Lord, may I remember that You Yourself are God in heaven above and on the earth below, and that there is none other besides You. May I keep myself from every form of idolatry.

MEDITATION PASSAGE FOR TODAY:

verses 6–9, 24, 35, 37, 39

The Ten Commandments were previously revealed in Exodus 20, and Moses reviews them here for the sake of the new generation that is being prepared to conquer the promised land. These commandments were not designed to oppress the people but to give them the freedom of appropriate boundaries in their relationships with God and with each other. God always wants what is best for His people: "Oh that they had such a heart in them, that they would fear Me and keep all My commandments always, that it may be well with them and with their sons forever!" The Lord's desire is that His children would enjoy life by ordering their steps according to His good ways.

READING OF DEUTERONOMY 5

Prayer:

Lord, I know that You always want what is best for Your people and that You desire us to cling firmly to You and not stray from the way that leads to life. Give me the power to walk in the Spirit and so fulfill Your royal law.

MEDITATION PASSAGE FOR TODAY:

verses 24, 29, 33

I n giving His commandments, the Lord sought the well-being and longevity of His people. When they loved Him with all their hearts, it would spill over into their homes and into their habits. He warned them that their prosperity could cause them to forget that He is the source of all their benefits. God gave the children of Israel His commandments, testimonies, and statutes so that it would be well with them. His purpose in bringing them *out* of Egypt was to bring them *in* to the promised land and to bless them with abundance and every good thing.

READING OF DEUTERONOMY 6

Prayer:

Lord, the things You command Your people to do are always in our best interests. Help me remember that You are never the enemy of my joy and well-being, but rather that You are the Source of all that is best for me.

MEDITATION PASSAGE FOR TODAY:

verses 4–7, 23

DAY 52—DEUTERONOMY 7

The Lord underscored the importance of not participating in the heathen practices of the nations the Israelites were sent to conquer. His people were not to intermarry with the nations but were to sustain their separate identity as a holy community that was dedicated to God. They were to remain "a people for His own possession out of all the peoples who are on the face of the earth." The Lord reminded them that He did not set His love on them because of their size or virtue, but because He simply chose to do so. His desire was to bless them in all ways, but this would depend on whether they remained faithful to Him.

READING OF DEUTERONOMY 7

Prayer:

Lord, I am thankful that the love You bestowed on Your people was not elicited by anything they had achieved or merited. Since Your love is unearned, I cannot diminish or increase it, and therefore I am secure in Your grace.

MEDITATION PASSAGE FOR TODAY:

verses 6–9

The theme of remembrance recurs often in the Old Testament, because God knows that embedded in human nature is a tendency to forget. It seems that nothing ages more quickly than gratitude, and that given a little time, people have a way of reducing grace to entitlement. Therefore Moses exhorted the generation of the conquest to remember God's benefits and not to slip into the arrogance of autonomy in which they supposed in their heart, "My power and the strength of my hand made me this wealth." Instead, it is the Lord God who gave them the power to make wealth; if they forgot this, He could just as easily take it away.

READING OF DEUTERONOMY 8

Prayer:

Lord, I ask for the grace to remember all of Your benefits and to realize that everything I have comes from You, though I may be tempted to slip into the delusion that I achieved these things without You.

MEDITATION PASSAGE FOR TODAY:

verses 3, 18

After reviewing the commandments, testimonies, and statutes with the new generation, Moses instructed them to write all the words of the law on large whitewashed stones after they crossed the Jordan River so that they would serve as an altar and a reminder about the covenant commitment they had entered into with the Lord their God. It was essential for their well-being that they obey the voice of the Lord and observe His commandments. Six of the tribes were to proclaim blessings for obedience from Mount Gerizim, and six of the tribes were to proclaim cursings for disobedience from Mount Ebal.

READING OF DEUTERONOMY 27

Prayer:

Lord, You are serious about the things You exhort Your children to know, be, and do. Let me realize with greater clarity the blessings of obedience and the consequences of disobedience.

MEDITATION PASSAGE FOR TODAY:

verse 10

DAY 55—DEUTERONOMY 28

The list of blessings for obedience in the theocratic covenant community is impressive, extending to every realm of life: physical, economic, social, and political. However, the list of cursings for disobedience in the same community of faith is equally impressive, and just as pervasive. It is clear that to whom much as been given, much will be required. Sadly, Moses knew which way the people would eventually turn, and that the Lord would scatter the people of Israel among the nations because of their disobedience to His covenant.

READING OF DEUTERONOMY 28

Prayer:

Lord, this list of blessings and cursings is a sober reminder to me that right now counts forever, and that the quality of my walk with You in this life will have an impact on the rewards I receive when I stand to give an account to Your Son.

MEDITATION PASSAGE FOR TODAY:

verses 1, 58

N earing the end of his lengthy discourse to the people, Moses reminds them that it is the Lord who established His covenant with them and that they entered into it willingly. The Lord's desire was to establish them as a people for Himself, but Moses made it clear that they would eventually forsake the Lord their God and experience the devastating adversity consequent to serving other gods. This chapter is a reminder that "God is not mocked; for whatever a man sows, this he will also reap" (Galatians 6:7).

READING OF DEUTERONOMY 29

Prayer:

Lord, I know that this life is not a dress rehearsal but is very real in its nature and consequences. By Your grace, I want to make my time count for eternity by treasuring You and obeying the things You ask me to do.

MEDITATION PASSAGE FOR TODAY:

verses 9, 13, 29

M oses concludes his sermons to the people by predicting not only their future captivity among the nations where the Lord would drive them, but also their future repentance and restoration from captivity. He leaves them with the choice between life and death, good and evil, blessing and cursing, along with the consequences of that choice to love God or to abandon Him. Moses urges his people to love God, obey His voice, and cling to Him so that they will dwell and prosper in the land.

READING OF DEUTERONOMY 30

Prayer:

Lord, You dealt with Israel by relating material benefits and loss to obedience and disobedience. I realize that in the body of Christ, the blessings for obedience relate more to the fruit of the Spirit than to the fruit of the vine. Let me walk by Your Spirit and enjoy His benefits.

MEDITATION PASSAGE FOR TODAY:

verses 11–16, 19–20

Day 58—Deuteronomy 32

T he song of Moses was a sad and realistic indictment against the people that reminded them of their rich heritage and their repeated tendency to forget the God who fathered them. Their idolatry provoked the Lord to jealousy, since He wanted His people to be wholly His. "See now that I, I am He, and there is no god besides Me; it is I who put to death and give life. I have wounded and it is I who heal, and there is no one who can deliver from My hand." Obedience to God's words was their very life, but disobedience and rebellion would lead to death.

READING OF DEUTERONOMY 32

Prayer:

Lord, my life is hidden with You in the heavenly places in Christ. May I look to Christ, abide in Him, and draw my sustenance from Him in all things.

MEDITATION PASSAGE FOR TODAY:

verses 4, 39

M oses blessed the children of Israel before going up to Mount Nebo to die. After reminding them of the Lord's great love for them, this humble servant of the Lord was granted a miraculous vision of the entire promised land even as far as the Mediterranean Sea. The Lord Himself buried Moses in an unmarked place, and his protégé Joshua was endued with the spirit of wisdom in his earlier commissioning when Moses had laid his hands on him. Moses enjoyed a unique relationship with the Lord, in that the Lord knew him face to face.

READING OF DEUTERONOMY 34

Prayer:

Lord, I am grateful for Your dedicated and obedient servant Moses. I thank You that You continue to use us, in spite of our lapses, when we return to You. I ask for the grace of fidelity to You and Your purposes.

MEDITATION PASSAGE FOR TODAY:

verses 10–12

Day 60—Joshua 1

As soon as Joshua assumed the mantle of Moses, he faced the daunting task of leading the children of Israel across the Jordan River to begin their conquest of the promised land. The Lord Himself encouraged Joshua and exhorted him to be strong and of good courage. Further, the key to Joshua's success rested in his relationship with the Lord, and therefore he needed to be a man of the Word who meditated in it day and night. By cultivating his daily walk with God, Joshua would be a fit leader to guide the people into the inheritance the Lord had promised to them.

READING OF JOSHUA 1

Prayer:

Lord, thank You for the wealth of Your Word. Like Joshua, I want to be shaped by Your Word and keep it before me so that I will observe to do according to all that is written in it.

MEDITATION PASSAGE FOR TODAY:

verses 7–9

The story of Rahab the harlot is a remarkable account of a woman who knew little about the God of Israel, but who applied the little she knew. Rahab took the risk of protecting the two Israelite spies who came to investigate the city of Jericho. When she hid them on the roof of her house on the city wall, she acknowledged to them that the "the LORD your God, He is God in heaven above and on earth beneath." She asked for the reward of protection when Israel overtook her city, and they instructed her to bind a line of scarlet cord in her window as a token against that day. She and her household were spared (Joshua 6). She is mentioned in Matthew 1 as being a part of the Messianic line and in Hebrews 11 and James 2 as an example of faith in action.

READING OF JOSHUA 2

Prayer:

Lord, I thank You for the example of simple faith in the life of this Gentile woman who put her complete trust in You. Thank You for honoring those who honor You.

MEDITATION PASSAGE FOR TODAY:

verse 11

Joshua demonstrated his leadership and confidence in the Lord in this account of the crossing of the Jordan River. The Lord established Joshua's authority in the eyes of the children of Israel when Joshua obediently followed His instructions about commanding the priests to bear the ark of the covenant to the edge of the water. When the soles of the feet of the priests touched the overflowing waters of the river, the Lord cut off the flow of water until all the people were able to cross the riverbed on dry ground. Just as Moses led the people safely through the waters of the Red Sea, so his successor Joshua led them safely through the waters of the Jordan River.

READING OF JOSHUA 3

Prayer:

Lord, You are the supremely worthy object of trust, since You have demonstrated the truth of Your promises again and again in the Old and New Testament history of redemption. Let me remember Your wonderful works among the sons of men.

MEDITATION PASSAGE FOR TODAY:

verse 10

The Lord instructed Joshua to memorialize the miraculous crossing of the Jordan River on dry ground by appointing representatives from each of the twelve tribes to carry a stone from the midst of the Jordan riverbed to Gilgal beyond the western shore. In this way, the stones would be a sign to the generations to follow. In addition, Joshua had the people set up twelve stones in the midst of the Jordan before the waters returned. When the priests came up from the riverbed, the waters of the Jordan returned and once again overflowed the banks. Thus, Joshua's authority was permanently established among the people.

READING OF JOSHUA 4

Prayer:

Lord, I thank You that You have demonstrated that Your hand is mighty and that we should fear You forever. You have accomplished great things for Your people, and all Your ways are righteous and true.

MEDITATION PASSAGE FOR TODAY:

verses 14, 24

After Joshua had an encounter with the Commander of the army of the Lord at the end of Joshua 5, he received the Lord's instructions as to how to conquer the walled city of Jericho. Everything about this conquest was unorthodox; it is significant that while the later battles under Joshua demonstrate great military tactics, this first battle had to be won solely by faith and obedience to the Lord. Thus, it would be clear from the outset that all the battles of Joshua had to be fought in the Lord's strength and not in dependence on human skill and abilities. God honored Israel's obedience to His apparently strange instructions, and this was one of the great moments in Israel's history.

READING OF JOSHUA 6

Prayer:

Lord, this account speaks to me about the whole nature of living the spiritual life. I realize how tempting it is to depend upon my own skill and abilities, when in fact I must always walk in childlike trust and obedience, looking to You for the victory.

MEDITATION PASSAGE FOR TODAY:

verse 27

N earing the end of his life, Joshua called the elders and leaders of Israel to give them a final message of exhortation and encouragement to remain faithful to the ways of the Lord. He reminded them that it is the Lord who fought for them, and that their relationship to the Lord will be determinative of their continued success in the land. They needed the courage to keep and to do all that is written in the Book of the Law of Moses, and to love the Lord. Otherwise they would descend into the morass of idolatry and intermarry with the remnant of the nations they were called to conquer. Just as the Lord has been faithful to them, so they must be faithful to Him.

READING OF JOSHUA 23

Prayer:

Lord, without fidelity to the spiritual disciplines of prayer and of time in Your Word, I will be vulnerable to the lures of this world system and tempted to turn away from You as my first love. May I hold fast to You and love You above all things.

MEDITATION PASSAGE FOR TODAY:

verses 6, 14

M any begin well and end poorly, but Joshua finished his race well and remained faithful to the Lord throughout his one hundred and ten years. In his message to the leaders of his people, Joshua reminded them of the Lord's gracious and powerful works on behalf of the children of Israel and in the past until the present day. With this perspective fresh in their minds, Joshua moved into application by exhorting his countrymen to fear the Lord, to serve Him in sincerity and truth, and to put away all forms of idolatry. Joshua warned the people that the Lord is a jealous God who will not endure faithlessness or rebellion, but they vowed to serve the Lord, and Joshua made a covenant with them.

READING OF JOSHUA 24

Prayer:

Lord, it is clear that the only options before me are service to You or service to idolatry by putting anything in the created order higher in my affections and priorities than You. Help me remember that You are a jealous God who will not let Your children stray away from You without being disciplined.

MEDITATION PASSAGE FOR TODAY:

verses 14–15

D uring the days of the judges, "there was no king in Israel; every man did what was right in his own eyes" (Judges 17:6). This book records the results of turning away from the Lord through apostasy, idolatry, and immorality. After the generations of Joshua and the elders who outlived Joshua, the children of Israel succumbed to the lure of idolatry and served the gods of the surrounding nations. They went through several cycles that moved from sin (idolatry) to servitude (oppression by a foreign power) to supplication (the people would finally cry to the Lord) to salvation (the Lord would raise up a deliverer-judge) to silence (a period of rest until the cycle began once again after the death of the judge).

READING OF JUDGES 2

Prayer:

Lord, the cycles in the book of Judges illustrate the monotony of sin and the creativity of Your saving works on behalf of Your people. May I not linger under sin's dominion, but quickly return to You when I fall into disobedience.

MEDITATION PASSAGE FOR TODAY:

verse 7

When the Lord raised up the Midianites to oppress the people of Israel due to their unfaithfulness to Him, they finally cried out to God after seven years. In response, the Lord sent a prophet who rebuked them for their infidelity and also sent the Angel of the Lord to commission Gideon to become Israel's deliverer from the power of the Midianites. Gideon followed the Lord's instructions to tear down the altar of Baal and to build an altar to the Lord. Gideon sent messengers to gather an army to defeat the Midianites and requested two evidences to assure himself that he was indeed being called by the Lord.

READING OF JUDGES 6

Prayer:

Lord, twice You condescended to respond to Gideon's request for a sign. I thank You that You do not wait until our faith is perfect before You call us, but that You gradually reveal Yourself to those who truly want to know You.

MEDITATION PASSAGE FOR TODAY:

verses 22–23

K nowing the human tendency to depend upon our own resources rather than trust in the Lord, God instructed Gideon to reduce the size of his army by allowing those who were fearful to return home. Even so, the ten thousand who remained were still too numerous, so the Lord reduced their number to three hundred. Now that the odds were impossible, it was time for the Lord to act. Once again, God gave Gideon a sign to encourage him. Then when the three hundred blew their trumpets and broke their pitchers, holding torches in their left hands and trumpets in their right hands, the Lord completely routed the Midianite armies. Thus it was the sword of the Lord that defeated their enemies.

READING OF JUDGES 7

Prayer:

Lord, I realize that it is not possible for me to wage spiritual warfare effectively in the power of the flesh. Help me remember to stand firm in Christ, to submit to You, and to resist the world, the flesh, and the devil in Your strength.

MEDITATION PASSAGE FOR TODAY:

verse 2

A s the visit of the Angel of the Lord to Manoah and his wife in Judges 13 makes clear, Samson was set apart to the Lord before he was conceived. It was through this remarkable figure that the Lord began to deliver Israel out of the hand of the Philistines. Samson's penchant for foreign women provided an occasion to move against the Philistines. In this chapter, the Spirit of the Lord came mightily upon Samson when he was attacked by a lion and when he went down to Ashkelon to kill thirty of the Philistines.

READING OF JUDGES 14

Prayer:

Lord, You are able to accomplish Your purposes in spite of human shortcomings. Though Samson was physically powerful, he was frail in character, and it was only in the power of Your Spirit that he prevailed.

MEDITATION PASSAGE FOR TODAY:

verse 4

Day 71—Judges 15

I n his anger in losing his Philistine wife, Samson wreaked havoc by releasing three hundred foxes with torches tied between their tails in the grain fields, vineyards, and olive groves of the Philistines. When they responded by burning Samson's former wife and father-in-law, Samson slaughtered many of the Philistines. Samson allowed his fearful Israelite countrymen to tie him with new ropes and deliver him into the hands of the Philistines, but the Spirit of the Lord came mightily upon him, so that he killed a thousand of them with the jawbone of a donkey.

READING OF JUDGES 15

Prayer:

Lord, You fulfill Your plans through varied and unexpected means. The very strangeness of this account reminds me that Your ways among the sons of men are surprising and unpredictable.

MEDITATION PASSAGE FOR TODAY:

verses 14, 19

DAY 72—JUDGES 16

Once again, Samson had a liaison with a Philistine woman, and again the Lord delivered him from a death trap. The miracle of his uprooting and carrying the huge city gate of Gaza over thirty miles to Hebron is understated.

Samson's final relationship with a Philistine woman led to his downfall. Delilah was a persuasive and persistent woman who would not cease to manipulate him until she discovered the source of his strength so she could sell him into the hands of the Philistine lords. Each time, Samson came closer to the truth, until he made the fatal mistake of revealing his secret and presuming that God would once again deliver him. Nevertheless, Samson was allowed to have a final victory against three thousand of his enemies.

READING OF JUDGES 16

Prayer:

Lord, this tragic story makes me wonder about the potential of this man had he walked in obedience to Your ways. I realize that more often than not, You use us in spite of ourselves and not because of our abilities. Let me remember to walk in Your strength and not in my own.

MEDITATION PASSAGE FOR TODAY:

verses 28, 30

The story of Ruth and Boaz is a beautiful cameo of character, courage, and commitment during the days of the judges. It is a gem whose brilliance is enhanced by contrast to the darkness of the backdrop when "every man did what was right in his own eyes" (Judges 17:6).

Because of a famine in Bethlehem ("house of bread"), Elimelech took his wife Naomi and their two sons across the Jordan River to the country of Moab. After losing her husband and sons, Naomi decided to return to Bethlehem since the famine had broken. Ruth, one of her Moabite daughters-in-law, refused to remain in Moab but risked everything out of love for Naomi and followed her to Bethlehem.

READING OF RUTH 1

Prayer:

Lord, I thank You for the love of Ruth for Naomi and for her willingness to say, "Your people shall be my people, and your God, my God." May I too abandon myself to You and Your loving purposes.

MEDITATION PASSAGE FOR TODAY:

verses 16–17

DAY 74—RUTH 2

The sovereign and purposeful hand of God is behind each of the scenes in the Book of Ruth. When Ruth sought to glean in the fields after the reapers, she "happened" to come to the portion of the field belonging to Naomi's kinsman Boaz. Impressed by what he had heard about Ruth's commitment to her mother-in-law, Boaz promised to protect her. In addition, Boaz provided for her through his instructions to his men, and it was obvious to Naomi when Ruth returned from the field that someone took notice of her. When she heard it was her kinsman Boaz, the formerly embittered Naomi blessed the Lord for His kindness.

READING OF RUTH 2

Prayer:

Lord, this wonderful story reminds me that You are at work in ways I cannot predict or imagine. When I am tempted to be embittered at my circumstances, let me remember that You are working all things together for my good and that the only safe refuge is under Your wings.

MEDITATION PASSAGE FOR TODAY:

verses 12, 20

Naomi was a shrewd woman who analyzed the situation and knew what had to be done. She instructed her daughter-in-law to dress up and wait until Boaz had finished eating and drinking in celebration of the barley harvest. Then she was to cast herself on his mercy under cover of darkness and await his response. Ruth obediently followed Naomi's instructions; when Boaz discovered her at his feet at midnight, he blessed her for not going after younger men. He would act as her *goel*, her kinsman-redeemer, if her nearer kinsman would not perform this duty for her. Before sending her back to Naomi, Boaz gave Ruth a generous supply of barley.

READING OF RUTH 3

Prayer:

Lord, the drama of this chapter points beyond itself to the greatest drama of Your creative and redemptive work on behalf of the people upon whom You have set Your love. Like Ruth, let me be obedient to the role You call me to play.

MEDITATION PASSAGE FOR TODAY:

verses 10–11

A s Naomi predicted, Boaz would not rest until he conclud-
ed the matter of redeeming the land Naomi had sold and
marrying Ruth. Since there was a nearer kinsman, Boaz first
had to offer the right of redemption to him, and this must have
been a tense moment for him, since he had come to love Ruth.
At first the nearer kinsman agreed to redeem the land, but then
declined when he found he would also have to raise an inheritance through Ruth. Boaz then formalized his commitment to
act as Ruth's kinsman-redeemer before the elders at the city
gate, and they blessed him. Significantly, Obed, the son of Ruth
and Boaz, would become the grandfather of King David.

READING OF RUTH 4

Prayer:

*Lord, I thank You that this story which began in tragedy and
apparent hopelessness ended in joy and hope. In Your grace,
You took this Gentile woman and made her a direct part of the
Messianic line. You accomplish far more abundantly beyond all
that we ask or think.*

MEDITATION PASSAGE FOR TODAY:

verses 11–12, 14

H annah's grief in being barren was amplified by the taunts she received year after year by her rival Peninnah, the other wife of Elkanah. It was particularly painful when she had to go up to the house of the Lord in Jerusalem each year with the rest of the family. In her bitterness of soul, she prayed to the Lord and made a vow that if the Lord granted her the gift of a son, she would dedicate him to the Lord's service. When Eli the priest realized her anguish, he blessed her and said, "may the God of Israel grant your petition that you have asked of Him." The Lord fulfilled her request, and Hannah fulfilled her vow by presenting the child for the Lord's service after she had weaned him.

READING OF 1 SAMUEL 1

Prayer:

Lord, I thank You that You care for us and are concerned with the things that concern us. May I be anxious for nothing, but in everything by prayer and supplication, with thanksgiving, I will make my requests known to You.

MEDITATION PASSAGE FOR TODAY:

verses 10, 17

H annah's prayer of thanksgiving, similar to the *Magnificat* of Mary in Luke 1, is one of the great prayers of the Bible. She extols the name and character of the Lord and acknowledges His sovereignty over all things. The Lord later granted her the gift of sons and daughters because of her faithfulness.

By contrast, the sons of Eli were unfaithful priests whose wickedness desecrated the sanctuary of the Lord. The Lord sent a man of God to rebuke Eli for his failure to discipline his sons. Because he dishonored the Lord in this way, the Lord would judge him and his sons.

READING OF 1 SAMUEL 2

Prayer:

Lord, Your Word reveals the entire range of human character from fidelity and integrity to rebellion and treachery. Let me remember that You honor those who honor You, and that those who despise You will be lightly esteemed.

MEDITATION PASSAGE FOR TODAY:

verses 2, 6–7, 30

"Now the boy Samuel was growing in stature and in favor both with the LORD and with men" (1 Samuel 2:26; cf. Luke 2:52). As a lad, Samuel ministered to the Lord before Eli, and on one significant night, he heard the voice of the Lord. Thinking Eli had called him, he ran to Eli who sent him back. After this happened three times, Eli realized that the voice was that of the Lord and told Samuel to say, "Speak, LORD, for Your servant is listening." The Lord gave Samuel a message of judgment for Eli, and Samuel reluctantly relayed this prophetic message of condemnation.

READING OF 1 SAMUEL 3

Prayer:

Lord, I acknowledge Your holiness and my need to treat You as holy and not besmirch Your name in the sight of others by allowing sin to reign in my life.

MEDITATION PASSAGE FOR TODAY:

verse 19

I t is ironic that when Samuel grew old, his two sons became as treacherous and rebellious as Eli's two sons had been when Samuel was a boy. The people of Israel did not want Samuel's sons to succeed him as judges but instead clamored for a king to rule over them like all the nations. Thus, Israel rejected the theocracy and opted for a monarchy. Samuel warned them of the consequences of this action and what it would cost them to submit to the authority of an earthly king. But the people refused to listen to Samuel's warning and insisted on having a visible king to judge them and fight their battles. The Lord instructed Samuel to listen to them and grant their request.

READING OF 1 SAMUEL 8

Prayer:

Lord, I realize that it is easy to clamor for things You know are not best for me. By Your grace, protect me from myself so that I will not pursue something I will later live to regret.

MEDITATION PASSAGE FOR TODAY:

verses 7–8

The Lord had already selected the man whom Samuel would anoint as Israel's first king. Saul was a handsome, tall, and imposing figure who had all the appearance and potential of an impressive ruler. God used the incident of Kish's lost donkeys as a means of drawing Saul to seek out Samuel the seer. Before Saul arrived, the Lord told Samuel that He was sending him the man he was to anoint as ruler over the people. Samuel sat Saul in the place of honor at the feast and later talked with him to prepare him to hear the word of God for him.

READING OF 1 SAMUEL 9

Prayer:

Lord, what appears to me to be happenstance can be Your divine arrangements for new directions of which I have no knowledge. Let me be sensitive and responsive to Your guidance so that I will not miss what You have for me.

MEDITATION PASSAGE FOR TODAY:

verse 16

S amuel took Saul aside and privately anointed him with a flask of oil to be the ruler over the Lord's inheritance. In specific terms, Samuel predicted the immediate course of events and instructed Saul as to what to do. A transforming moment would take place when the Spirit of the Lord would come upon him and turn him into another man. After the Spirit of God came upon Saul and he prophesied among the prophets, Samuel called the people together to behold the man God had set apart to become their king. When they saw his impressive appearance, they shouted and said, "Long live the king!"

READING OF 1 SAMUEL 10

Prayer:

Lord, keep me from looking at people and circumstances from an outward and superficial perspective. I ask that the mind of Christ would grow in me, and that I would come to see things more from a biblical perspective.

MEDITATION PASSAGE FOR TODAY:

verses 6, 19

King Saul began well, but it did not take him long to slip into the sin of disobedience by buckling under outward pressure (1 Samuel 13). Samuel later gave Saul specific instructions to utterly destroy Amalek and all that he had, but Saul made the presumptuous decision to redefine the Lord's commands by sparing Agag and saving the best of the spoil. This act of rebellion marked the turning point in Saul's life, and the hand of the Lord was no longer upon him. In spite of Saul's excuses and sorrow, the kingdom would be torn from him and given to a better man who would obey the Lord.

READING OF 1 SAMUEL 15

Prayer:

Lord, I see the danger in rationalizing disobedience by redefining Your commands. Please keep me from the sins of presumption and rebellion so that I will walk in the obedience of humility.

MEDITATION PASSAGE FOR TODAY:

verses 22–23, 29

N ow that Saul had disqualified himself as God's anointed ruler over the people of Israel, the Lord instructed Samuel to go and anoint the man who would replace him as king. When Samuel was sent to Bethlehem to determine which of Jesse's sons God had selected to replace Saul as king, he looked at Eliab and assumed that he must be the Lord's anointed. But God told Samuel, "Do not look at his appearance or at the height of his stature, because I have rejected him; for God sees not as man sees, for man looks at the outward appearance, but the LORD looks at the heart." It was David, Jesse's youngest son, who was destined for the throne, and David soon began to serve Saul.

READING OF 1 SAMUEL 16

Prayer:

Lord, without You it is impossible for me to see things as they truly are. Since I can only judge on the basis of outward appearance, I ask that You would guide my decisions and direction.

MEDITATION PASSAGE FOR TODAY:

verse 7

The Philistine threat loomed large when they put forward a giant of a champion to discourage and taunt the armies of Israel. Goliath's defiant challenge brought great fear in the Israelite camp, and no one was willing to rise to fight the giant. When David heard about this, he was dismayed that this Philistine was successfully defying the armies of the living God. David's complete trust in the Lord gave him a confidence and perspective that the rest of his countrymen lacked. He told Goliath that the Lord would deliver him into his hand, and his defeat of Goliath encouraged the men of Israel and Judah to pursue the Philistines to their own territory.

READING OF 1 SAMUEL 17

Prayer:

Lord, this thrilling story reminds me once again that it is not the size of my opposition that matters but the power of my God. Let me walk in dependence upon the power of Your Spirit and put my confidence entirely in You.

MEDITATION PASSAGE FOR TODAY:

verses 26, 36, 46

A fter the death of King Saul, David was publicly anointed in Hebron as king over Judah and Benjamin. The northern ten tribes of Israel, however, continued for seven years and six months to support the house of Saul, but the house of David continued to grow in strength. With the death of Saul's son Ishbosheth, the ten tribes of Israel gathered at Hebron and anointed David as king over all Israel. David defeated the Jebusites and made Jerusalem his capital city. He then decisively defeated Israel's long-standing Philistine enemies by inquiring of the Lord and obediently carrying out God's instructions.

READING OF 2 SAMUEL 5

Prayer:

Lord, Your servant David illustrates the fact that patient obedience and dependence on You is the pathway of life. May I wait upon You, depend upon Your timing and strength, and obey all that You tell me to do.

MEDITATION PASSAGE FOR TODAY:

verses 2, 12

After David had firmly established his kingdom and attained rest from his enemies, his thoughts turned to honoring the Lord by building a permanent temple in Jerusalem to replace the tabernacle that had been built in the days of Moses. But the Lord told David through Nathan the prophet that it would not be him but his son after him who would build a house for His name. Instead of David building a house for God, it was God who would establish a house and a kingdom for David and for his descendants after him. David responded to this covenant God was making with him and his seed by praising the greatness of the Lord God and asking for God's name to be magnified forever.

READING OF 2 SAMUEL 7

Prayer:

Lord, I thank You for this Davidic Covenant, because it is perfectly fulfilled in the Person and work of the Lord Jesus. Indeed, in Jesus, the Root and the Offspring of David, You have established the throne of David's kingdom forever.

MEDITATION PASSAGE FOR TODAY:

verses 12–16, 22

D avid's victories over his enemies made him vulnerable to
the troubling question, "Where do I go from here?" The
middle-aged king decided not to lead his men in battle against
the Ammonites but to remain at the palace in Jerusalem while
Joab led his men instead. In his weakened spiritual condition,
he succumbed not only to the sin of adultery but also to the sin
of murder so that he could claim Bathsheba for himself. By dis-
posing of Uriah the Hittite, one of his thirty mighty men, David
supposed that he could get away with his sin.

READING OF 2 SAMUEL 11

Prayer:

*Lord, I realize that the flesh is neither improved nor removed
in this life, and that the one who thinks he stands should take
heed lest he fall. By Your grace, let me cultivate a passion for
Jesus so that I will not slip into despondency and succumb to
temptation.*

MEDITATION PASSAGE FOR TODAY:

verse 11

M onths passed and Bathsheba bore David a son. By this time, the king must have supposed that he had avoided the potential consequences of his sins against Bathsheba and her husband Uriah. But the Lord sent Nathan the prophet who related a parable that incited the king and exposed the extent of his hidden guilt. When he realized that the parable was actually about him, David repented (see Psalm 51) and acknowledged his sin against the Lord. Nathan told him that the consequences for his sin would be the loss of the child borne out of adultery as well as division in his own household. But the Lord in His grace comforted Bathsheba with another son, the great Solomon who would carry on the Davidic dynasty.

READING OF 2 SAMUEL 12

Prayer:

Lord, in Your grace and mercy, You are quick to forgive, but I pray that I will not presume on Your grace, supposing that I can get away with the consequences of folly. I know that You discipline those whom You love so that we will be partakers of Your holiness.

MEDITATION PASSAGE FOR TODAY:

verses 13–14, 23

A s David was declining, his kingdom was in jeopardy of usurpation by Adonijah. David had made it clear that Solomon was to be his successor (1 Chronicles 22), and Nathan the prophet was alarmed about this course of events that was taking place without David's knowledge. He quickly acted by arranging for Bathsheba to speak to David on behalf of Solomon and then appearing before the king himself. The king responded by arranging for Zadok the priest and Nathan the prophet to anoint Solomon king and to have him sit on David's throne before the people. When Adonijah saw that his plot to take the throne was defeated, he requested and received mercy from the new King Solomon.

READING OF 1 KINGS 1

Prayer:

Lord, in spite of multiplied human efforts to act independently of You and to refuse to heed Your Word, Your sovereign purposes are never thwarted by the devices and desires of men. I thank You that Your Word is truth, and that nothing can prevent it from being fulfilled.

MEDITATION PASSAGE FOR TODAY:

verses 29–30, 48

J ust before his death, David exhorted Solomon to remain faithful and obedient to the Lord, and he also instructed his son to deal with those who had troubled him. Adonijah, Solomon's older half-brother who had plotted to claim the throne made a foolish request through Bathsheba that led to his execution. Solomon also removed Abiathar from the priesthood for his infidelity to David and he executed Joab for defecting to Adonijah and for his earlier wickedness in murdering Abner and Amasa. Finally, Solomon restricted Shimei who had publicly cursed David and executed him when he violated the restriction. Thus, King Solomon firmly established his throne.

READING OF 1 KINGS 2

Prayer:

Lord, these men reaped what they had sown and received justice for their acts of treachery. But I ask You to treat me with mercy and not justice, and to preserve me in the grace of Your pardon.

MEDITATION PASSAGE FOR TODAY:

verse 3

When the Lord appeared to Solomon in a dream, He offered to grant Solomon one request. Solomon, aware of his own lack of experience and the burden of leadership that had been thrust upon him, requested an understanding heart to judge God's people with discernment. The Lord was pleased with this request for wisdom and told Solomon that he would not only be granted unprecedented wisdom, but that he would also receive what he had not asked. This great gift of wisdom was soon demonstrated publicly in Solomon's prudent judgment in the case of the two women who claimed the same child.

READING OF 1 KINGS 3

Prayer:

Lord, Solomon's humble request illustrates the truth that when we seek first Your kingdom and Your righteousness, the other needs of this life will be provided. Let me desire above all else the one thing most needful – the wisdom of trust in You.

MEDITATION PASSAGE FOR TODAY:

verses 9, 14

Day 93—1 Kings 8

King David had collected the materials necessary for the building of the temple, and it took Solomon seven years to construct and furnish it. The temple was a costly achievement of great beauty, a structure that must have been magnificent to behold. When Solomon gathered the elders of Israel to watch the priests bring the ark of the covenant into the Most Holy Place, the awesome glory of God filled the temple. Solomon then offered a sermon and a great prayer of dedication in which he entreated the Lord to hear the supplications of His people and to forgive their sins. This solemn prayer was followed by a time of rejoicing and celebration.

READING OF 1 KINGS 8

Prayer:

Lord, when I read about the early days of Solomon, I wish they could have lasted. But the joy, holiness, dignity, glory, and beauty that marked these days not only show what might have been had Your people remained faithful to You, but they also provide a hint of the far greater glory that is yet to be when You come to reign in righteousness.

MEDITATION PASSAGE FOR TODAY:

verses 27, 56

A fter the dedication of the temple, the Lord appeared to Solomon a second time and exhorted him to walk before Him in integrity of heart, uprightness, and obedience. The Lord made it clear that the temple was no talisman, and that He would destroy it if the people proved unfaithful to Him.

Solomon's many construction projects required forced labor, so the Canaanites who remained in the land were enslaved for this purpose. Solomon also built a fleet of merchant ships and generated huge revenues through extensive foreign trade.

READING OF 1 KINGS 9

Prayer:

Lord, this passage is like a parable of the tension between the temporal and eternal value systems. If I do not cling to You with a whole heart, my spiritual life will be choked by the cares of this world, the deceitfulness of riches, and the desires for other things.

MEDITATION PASSAGE FOR TODAY:

verses 4–5

According to the Abrahamic Covenant, it was through Abraham's descendants that all the families of the earth would be blessed. This account of Solomon and the queen of Sheba illustrates how this was beginning to happen during the righteous portion of Solomon's reign. When she came up to Jerusalem to test him with hard questions, Solomon's answers as well as the glory of his reign overwhelmed her. This was a rare instance in which the reality exceeded the rumors. Thus, this woman left Jerusalem with praise for the God of Israel: "Blessed be the LORD your God who delighted in you to set you on the throne of Israel; because the LORD loved Israel forever, therefore He made you king, to do justice and righteousness." Solomon's fame and wealth continued to increase.

READING OF 1 KINGS 10

Prayer:

Lord, this glorious scene shows what You intended for Your covenant nation. How short-lived are the days of righteousness, and how prone we are to turn away from You in times of prosperity. Let me remember how fleeting are my days on this earth, so that I will not spend them in vain.

MEDITATION PASSAGE FOR TODAY:

verse 9

The tragic contrast between chapters 10 and 11 could not be greater. Up until this point, Solomon demonstrated a heart for the Lord, but the seeds of his own downfall were beginning to spread as he sought to multiply horses, wives, and wealth in violation of the mandate for kings in Deuteronomy 17:14–20. Ironically, this wisest of men became a fool in his later years by succumbing to idolatry through the influence of his foreign wives. When Solomon turned his heart away from the Lord to other gods, the Lord told him that He would tear the northern kingdom away from his progeny. In addition, the Lord began to raise up foreign adversaries against Solomon, and Solomon's servant Jeroboam also rebelled against him.

READING OF 1 KINGS 11

Prayer:

Lord, it is easy to see the seeds of destruction in the tragic story of Solomon, but I ask that You would show me those subtle forces and patterns in my own life that could lead to my own downfall if I do not cling to You and remain faithful to You.

MEDITATION PASSAGE FOR TODAY:

verses 4, 9–10

T his chapter marks the transition in 931 B.C. from the united kingdom under Saul, David, and Solomon, to the divided kingdom of Israel in the north (ten tribes) and Judah in the south (two tribes). After the death of Solomon, his son Rehoboam foolishly rejected the prudent counsel of Jeroboam and the leaders of Israel to lighten the yoke his father had imposed upon them. The court officials affirmed the reasonableness of this request. Instead, Rehoboam listened to the shallow counsel of his peers who appealed to his pride. Rehoboam's harsh speech resulted in the revolt of the ten northern tribes who made Jeroboam king over Israel. Sadly, Jeroboam set up an idolatrous rival religion in Israel, fearing that he would lose power if his people continued to worship at the temple in Jerusalem.

READING OF 1 KINGS 12

Prayer:

Lord, the devastating consequences of foolish pride are evident in the lives of Rehoboam and Jeroboam. I ask that out of Your goodness You would make known to me, and take from my heart, every kind and form and degree of pride.

MEDITATION PASSAGE FOR TODAY:

verse 7

I n the days of Ahab, ruler of the northern kingdom of Israel, the Lord raised up the prophet Elijah to announce a drought because of Ahab's sin in bringing Baal worship to Israel through the influence of his wife Jezebel. The Lord provided for Elijah while he was in hiding by the brook Cherith, and then in the house of the widow Zarephath. The Lord miraculously replenished her flour and oil during the days of the drought, and revived her dead son through Elijah's prayers. With the restoration of her son, Zarephath knew that Elijah was a man of God who spoke the true word of the Lord.

READING OF 1 KINGS 17

Prayer:

Lord, You provide for Your people in the worst of circumstances and concern Yourself with the details of our lives. May I trust You more and lean on You during times of trial and adversity.

MEDITATION PASSAGE FOR TODAY:

verse 24

When the Lord sent Elijah to Ahab to end the drought, Elijah encountered Obadiah and told him to announce his return to Ahab. Obadiah, a godly man who had protected and provided for one hundred prophets in two caves when Jezebel massacred the prophets of the Lord, was afraid to tell Ahab until Elijah reassured him. Ahab went to meet with Elijah who challenged his false prophets to a contest on Mount Carmel. Elijah's dramatic single-handed victory over the four hundred and fifty prophets of Baal and the four hundred prophets of Asherah led to the people's cry, "The LORD, He is God; the LORD, He is God." Then Elijah prayed on the top of Carmel for the drought-breaking rain.

READING OF 1 KINGS 18

Prayer:

Lord, I thank You for the boldness of Your servant Elijah and for this remarkable account of Your power on behalf of those whose lives are dedicated to You. May I grow in holy boldness and proclaim the truth of Your Son in word and deed.

MEDITATION PASSAGE FOR TODAY:

verses 21, 37

Victory often produces vulnerability. After his spectacular public defeat of eight hundred and fifty false prophets, Elijah fled for his life when he received a threatening message from Queen Jezebel. In his depression and despair, Elijah was nourished by an angel as he headed south all the way to Mount Horeb. There in a cave on the mountain, the Lord gently dealt with him. The Lord was not in the violent wind or the earthquake or the fire, but He spoke to Elijah in a still small voice. The Lord instructed His despondent prophet to return north and anoint Hazael as king over Syria, Jehu as king over Israel, and Elisha as his successor.

READING OF 1 KINGS 19

Prayer:

Lord, I thank You for the gentle ways in which You encourage me in times of despondency. May I learn to fear and trust You rather than people, and may I have the courage to carry out Your commands to the honor of Your name.

MEDITATION PASSAGE FOR TODAY:

verses 11–13, 18

Ahaziah the son of Ahab followed the wicked ways of his father and continued the worship of Baal in Israel. When he was injured, the messengers he sent to inquire of the god Baal-Zebub were intercepted by Elijah who sent them back to Ahaziah to tell him the Lord said he would die. In his defiance, the king sent a band of soldiers to bring Elijah to him, but fire from heaven consumed them. This happened a second time, and the third group approached the prophet in humility and begged for their lives. Elijah went up with them and personally delivered the same message to Ahaziah who soon died according to Elijah's word.

READING OF 2 KINGS 1

Prayer:

Lord, what You decree no one can change or thwart. You judge unrighteousness and arrogance and lift up the humble. Let me remember to treat You as holy and to walk before You in loving fear.

MEDITATION PASSAGE FOR TODAY:

verse 16

W hen Elijah knew the Lord was about to take him into heaven by a whirlwind, he discouraged his protégé Elisha from following him to Bethel and then to Jericho. Elisha refused to leave him, and the prophets in both places realized that the Lord was about to take his master away. Significantly, the waters of the Jordan River parted to allow Elijah and Elisha to cross on dry ground, and before Elijah was taken up into heaven, Elisha asked for a double portion of his spirit. Elisha took up the mantle of Elijah, parted the waters of the river, and the prophets recognized that the spirit of Elijah rested on Elisha.

READING OF 2 KINGS 2

Prayer:

Lord, this amazing account of the way You took Your servant Elijah up to heaven in a chariot of fire and a whirlwind reminds me of how little I really know about You and how truly mysterious Your ways are to me. But I also know that the things You are preparing for me are also beyond my imagination, and that they will make the sufferings of this present life pale in comparison.

MEDITATION PASSAGE FOR TODAY:

verses 9–12

I t is evident in this and the following chapters that Elisha indeed received a double portion of Elijah's spirit. There are many parallels between the miracles of Elisha and those of our Lord, and the analogy has been made that Elijah is to Elisha as John the Baptist is to Jesus. Certainly the miracles of the increase of the widow's oil, the resuscitation of the Shunammite's son, the miracle of the deadly stew, and the multiplication of the loaves all foreshadow the miraculous ministry of the Lord Jesus. Elisha displayed compassion and concern for those around him and provided for their needs.

READING OF 2 KINGS 4

Prayer:

Lord, I am grateful for the ministry of Elisha and for the ways in which he typified Christ Jesus in his life and compassionate ministry. Thank You for the ways in which You have manifested Your character and nature through Your servants the prophets.

MEDITATION PASSAGE FOR TODAY:

verses 37, 44

W hen Naaman, commander of the army of the king of Syria, heard that there was a prophet in Israel who had the power to heal his leprosy, the king of Syria sent him with a letter to the king of Israel. The latter thought such a request was the Syrian king's way of seeking a quarrel with him, but Elisha assured him that he would deal with Naaman. At first Naaman balked when he was told by Gehazi, Elisha's servant, to wash in the Jordan seven times, but he humbled himself, followed the instructions, and was cured. Sadly, Gehazi saw this as an opportunity for material gain; then, because of his lie and his covetousness, he was struck with the leprosy of Naaman.

READING OF 2 KINGS 5

Prayer:

Lord, I thank You for this account of this Gentile's healing and conversion to You. I also thank You for the warning about the deceitfulness of the flesh and the lure of material gain. Let my character be free from covetousness so that I will be content with what I have.

MEDITATION PASSAGE FOR TODAY:

verse 8

E lisha continued to work signs and wonders, and one of his gifts was the knowledge of what the enemies of Israel were plotting. When the king of Syria heard that Elisha was thwarting his plans in this way, he sent an army to capture the prophet in Dothan. Elisha's servant was terrified to see the city surrounded, until Elisha prayed for him and he was granted a vision of God's protective forces. The Syrians were struck with blindness as Elisha led them to Samaria, Israel's capital, and then opened their eyes. But Elisha treated them with mercy and allowed them to return to Syria.

READING OF 2 KINGS 6

Prayer:

Lord, You empowered Your prophet Elisha to accomplish great things. I thank You for the way You raise up choice servants for significant ministries to comfort and provide for Your people, and I thank You that You continue to work through Your servants today.

MEDITATION PASSAGE FOR TODAY:

verses 16–17

B ecause of the Syrian siege of Samaria, the capital of Israel experienced such a severe famine that some of the people were resorting to cannibalism. The king of Israel blamed Elisha for the trouble and sought his life, but Elisha predicted that in the course of one day, the famine would be lifted. The Lord caused the Syrian army to hear the noise of a great army, and they fled in terror, leaving their provisions behind. When four lepers decided to surrender to the Syrians rather than starve in Samaria, they were amazed to see the empty camp and all the goods. They announced the good news to the gatekeepers of Samaria, and after a cautious investigation proved it was true, the people of the city plundered the empty Syrian tents.

READING OF 2 KINGS 7

Prayer:

Lord, there are no circumstances that are so severe that they cannot be overturned in an instant if You chose to do so. May I look at You and Your good pleasure rather than the circumstances I face, knowing that You will work all things together for good to those who love You and are called according to Your purpose.

MEDITATION PASSAGE FOR TODAY:

verses 6, 9

E lisha warned the Shunammite woman whose son he had restored to life about a seven-year famine the Lord was about to bring. The family sojourned in the land of the Philistines, and Elisha's servant was instrumental in the restoration of their land after their return.

When Ben-Hadad king of Syria sent Hazael to Elisha to inquire if he would recover from his illness, Elisha told Hazael he would become king of Syria and ravage the children of Israel. The chapter concludes with an account of the wickedness of Joram, king of Israel, and Jehoram and Ahaziah, kings of Judah. In the ninth chapter, Elisha anoints Jehu as king over Israel who executes both Joram and Ahaziah.

READING OF 2 KINGS 8

Prayer:

Lord, You are the Lord over history and the Judge of the rulers of the earth. Although the wicked often appear to gain the upper hand, You depose them in Your timing and raise up their replacements according to Your good pleasure. Your Word reminds me that although the unrighteous reign for a season, the righteous will reign with Christ forever.

MEDITATION PASSAGE FOR TODAY:

verses 11–13

A fter the death of the ungodly King Ahaz of Judah, his son Hezekiah assumed the throne and provided a window of righteous rule in the southern kingdom until Hezekiah's wicked son Manasseh succeeded him. King Hezekiah zealously removed the high places and objects of pagan worship and walked in the ways of the Lord God of Israel. It was in 722 B.C. during the reign of Hezekiah that the Assyrian King Shalmaneser finally overthrew the northern kingdom of Israel and scattered the people. After Hezekiah rebelled against the Assyrians, the Assyrian King Sennacherib sent forces to invade Judah, and Hezekiah relented by paying tribute. However, the Assyrians invaded Judah a second time and taunted Hezekiah for trusting in the God of Israel.

READING OF 2 KINGS 18

Prayer:

Lord, I know that there is no guarantee that righteousness will eliminate opposition and adversity in this life. Your enemies are ever active, but Yours is the power, majesty, glory, and victory, and I will put my trust and hope in You.

MEDITATION PASSAGE FOR TODAY:

verses 5–7

When Hezekiah heard Assyria's taunts through Rab-shakeh, he covered himself with sackcloth and went into the temple and sent a contingent of men to ask Isaiah the prophet to pray for the remnant of Judah. Isaiah assured them that the Lord would respond to this blasphemy and prophesied the overthrow of Sennacherib and the Assyrian army. Then in one night, the angel of the Lord killed one hundred and eighty-five thousand of the Assyrian army that was surrounding Jerusalem. The defeated Sennacherib returned to Nineveh where he was soon assassinated by two of his sons.

READING OF 2 KINGS 19

Prayer:

Lord, thank You for this account of Hezekiah's prayer, Isaiah's prophecy, and Your sudden and mighty deliverance of Your people in Jerusalem. Those who trust in You will overcome against impossible odds.

MEDITATION PASSAGE FOR TODAY:

verses 15–16, 19

When King Hezekiah was near death because of an illness, the prophet Isaiah told him he would not recover. But Hezekiah prayed to the Lord, and God instructed Isaiah to return and announce that He would grant the king an additional fifteen years of life. God gave Hezekiah a miraculous sign of his recovery, but not long after the king was healed, he foolishly and proudly displayed all of his treasures to a group of messengers from the king of Babylon. Because of this, Isaiah the prophet rebuked Hezekiah and prophesied that after his days, the Babylonians would carry away all of these treasures to their country.

READING OF 2 KINGS 20

Prayer:

Lord, even though You humbled Hezekiah through sickness, his heart succumbed to pride after he was cured. Please guard me from the subtle temptations to suppose that I can boast in anything other than You.

MEDITATION PASSAGE FOR TODAY:

verses 5–6

A fter a brief reform under Josiah, the last good king of the southern kingdom, a succession of four ungodly rulers finally led to the demise of the kingdom of Judah. Nebuchadnezzar, king of Babylon, invaded Judah in 605 B.C. and again in 597 B.C., carrying off captives on both occasions. But Nebuchadnezzar's third invasion in 586 B.C. marked the end of the kingdom of Judah when Nebuzaradan, captain of the guard, finally destroyed the city of Jerusalem, tore down its walls, burned the temple and the palace, and carried away the bulk of the people into captivity in Babylon. The few remaining people eventually went down to Egypt for fear of the Chaldeans.

READING OF 2 KINGS 25

Prayer:

Lord, it is sad to read this account of the ungodliness of the leaders and people of Judah and the consequent demise of Jerusalem, the temple, and the southern kingdom. May I remain aware of the destructive consequences of disobedience to You and hold fast to You in humility, sincerity, and truth.

MEDITATION PASSAGE FOR TODAY:

verses 8–11

After David's kingdom was established, he began the construction of his palace and arranged to move the ark of the covenant up to the City of David in Jerusalem. He appointed an order of worship for the tabernacle and soon desired to build a permanent temple where God would be worshiped and the ark of the covenant would be placed. The prophet Nathan told the king that the Lord would build David a lasting dynasty, and that David's son would be the one who would build the temple for the Lord. David responded in gratitude and praise for these covenant promises and asked that the Lord's name would be magnified through his descendants forever.

READING OF 1 CHRONICLES 17

Prayer:

Lord, I thank You for the promises of the Davidic Covenant and for Jesus, the Root and the Offspring of David, who fulfills these covenant blessings. I thank You that Jesus will reign over the house of Jacob forever, and of His kingdom there will be no end.

MEDITATION PASSAGE FOR TODAY:

verses 11–14, 20

DAY 113—1 CHRONICLES 29

C hronicles gives a later priestly perspective on the period of the kings, which is evident in the material in chapters 22 to 29. In this section of the book, detailed descriptions are given of the material provisions for the construction of the temple, the organization of the Levites and the priests, the orders of the temple musicians, the organization of the gatekeepers, the treasuries, and the temple officers, the leaders of the military divisions of Israel and of the twelve tribes, and the royal officers and counselors of David. The king gave his son Solomon the plans and provisions for the temple and offered a final prayer of thanksgiving before the coronation of his successor Solomon.

READING OF 1 CHRONICLES 29

Prayer:

Lord, the beauty, dignity, splendor, and order of Israel's worship at its peak in the reigns of David and Solomon were a great testimony to Your grace and power in transforming a people who were in bondage in Egypt and who wandered in the wilderness into a great and glorious nation.

MEDITATION PASSAGE FOR TODAY:

verses 10–19

N ear the end of the southern kingdom, the Lord raised up a last godly king whose righteousness led his people for a few years into a time of reform, prosperity, and joy. Josiah was only sixteen when he began to seek the God of his father David, and when he was twenty he began to purge the idolatrous images and altars from Judah and Jerusalem. At the age of twenty-six Josiah ordered the repair of the house of God. In the process, Hilkiah the high priest discovered the Book of the Law in the temple. When God's neglected Word was read to the king, Josiah realized that God's wrath must have been great because of the years of neglect and disobedience. Sadly, Josiah's reforms would come too late to avert divine judgment from Judah.

READING OF 2 CHRONICLES 34

Prayer:

Lord, it is amazing that Your Word was so neglected by Your people that it was actually lost for years. I ask that I will never take Your Word for granted, but that I will remain faithful to the disciplines of reading and meditating on Scripture.

MEDITATION PASSAGE FOR TODAY:

verses 21, 33

I n his responsiveness to the reading of the Book of the Law of Moses, King Josiah commanded that the people celebrate the Passover to the Lord for the first time in years. This was the greatest celebration of the Passover since the days of Samuel the prophet. Josiah was a capable leader whose passion and commitment for the Lord was contagious. He was able to rally the priests and the Levites and all Judah and Israel who were present. During his days, the people followed his lead by committing themselves to the Lord, but after his death, these reforms were quickly abandoned, and the people fell under the sway of a succession of four godless kings who brought the kingdom of Judah to ruin.

READING OF 2 CHRONICLES 35

Prayer:

Lord, this brief interlude of righteousness offers a cameo of what might have been had Your people remained faithful to You. Seeking their own interests above Yours, they brought about their own destruction. May I be careful to seek Your interests first.

MEDITATION PASSAGE FOR TODAY:

verses 16–18

The Book of Ezra contains the stories of the first two returns of the Jewish exiles at the conclusion of the Babylonian captivity. Ezra 1–6 portrays the first return led by Zerubbabel and the construction of the second temple in Jerusalem (536–516 B.C.). Ezra 7–10 presents the second return led by Ezra and the reformation of the people under his leadership (458–457 B.C.). With the decree of Cyrus king of Persia (559–530 B.C.), the Jewish people were granted permission to return to their land and to rebuild the house of the Lord in Jerusalem. Moreover, Cyrus returned the temple articles that had been taken by the Babylonians so that the captives could use them in the new temple.

READING OF EZRA 1

Prayer:

Lord, You are sovereign over the empires of this earth, and You use their rulers to accomplish Your purposes. I thank You that You never abandoned Your people, but preserved a remnant who could return to the land and continue the Messianic line.

MEDITATION PASSAGE FOR TODAY:

verses 2–3

In spite of fear of reprisal, Jeshua and Zerubbabel gathered the remnant and built the altar of the God of Israel so that the people could once again offer sacrifices to the Lord. They also celebrated the Feast of Tabernacles and began work on the foundation of the second temple in accordance with the decree issued by Cyrus king of Persia. When the builders completed the temple foundation, the priests celebrated with instruments and music to praise the Lord, singing responsively, "For He is good, for His lovingkindness is upon Israel forever." However, the shouts of joy were mingled with weeping by the older people who could remember the greater glory of the first temple.

READING OF EZRA 3

Prayer:

Lord, Your covenant faithfulness to Your people is great, and Your mercies never cease. Nevertheless, this text discloses the long-term consequences of disobedience and the loss of past blessings. Yet You promise that in Your grace, the best is yet to come.

MEDITATION PASSAGE FOR TODAY:

verse 11

T he adversaries of Judah and Benjamin sought to discourage the work on the new temple, but under the firm leadership of Zerubbabel and Jeshua they tried to continue. But their opponents were persistent, and this ongoing problem of attempting to prevent the Jewish people from being well-established in the land continued. This is evident in the account in the second part of Ezra 4 of later opposition under Artaxerxes king of Persia (464–423 B.C.) when the Jews first attempted to rebuild the walls of Jerusalem. The opponents of the Jewish people sent an alarming letter to Artaxerxes who responded by instructing them to make the Jews cease their work on the walls. The chapter ends by bringing us back to the time of Zerubbabel and the discontinuation of the work on the temple.

READING OF EZRA 4

Prayer:

Lord, it is not always clear to us why You allow godless agendas and spiritual warfare to delay Your work in this world, but I know that I can always trust You for the outcome, no matter how difficult the journey may seem.

MEDITATION PASSAGE FOR TODAY:

verse 3

The second temple was begun under Zerubbabel's leadership in 536 B.C., discontinued in 534 B.C., and not resumed until 520 B.C. when the prophets Haggai and Zechariah exhorted the Jewish people to complete the temple. Inspired by these prophets, Zerubbabel and Jeshua resumed the work. Immediately their opponents challenged them and asked them who gave them the right to resume. They refused to cease unless Darius the king of Persia (521–486 B.C.) issued an edict to this effect. When the opponents of the Jews wrote to Darius, they referred to the Jewish claim that Cyrus had issued a decree to build the temple and asked that a search be made for such a decree.

READING OF EZRA 5

Prayer:

Lord, the pressures of this world and its systems often discourage Your people from pressing on in obedience. May I remember that all who desire to live godly in Christ Jesus will suffer persecution, and may I take courage, knowing that You have overcome the world.

MEDITATION PASSAGE FOR TODAY:

verses 5, 11

K ing Darius responded to the letter sent by the opponents of the temple construction by ordering that a search be made in the archives for the alleged decree of Cyrus that the Jews build their temple. Providentially, a scroll was found that contained this decree, and this led Darius to command that the very people who opposed the temple construction assist in providing the means for its completion. Thus encouraged by this decree and the prophetic ministry of Haggai and Zechariah, the children of Israel completed their temple in 516 B.C. They joyfully celebrated the dedication of the temple and later celebrated the Passover at the new house of God in Jerusalem.

READING OF EZRA 6

Prayer:

Lord, You use even Your opponents to accomplish Your good pleasure. I thank You that You provide for Your people through unexpected means and that we can confidently look to You rather than fear opposition.

MEDITATION PASSAGE FOR TODAY:

verses 10, 16, 22

The first return of the Jews from their Babylonian captivity was led by Zerubbabel and is chronicled in Ezra 1–6 (538–516 B.C.). Ezra led the second return of the Jews in 457 B.C. (Ezra 7–10). The Book of Nehemiah records the third return led by Nehemiah (444–c. 425 B.C.). While Zerubbabel, Haggai, and Zechariah were concerned with the building of the second temple, Nehemiah focused decades later on the rebuilding of the walls around the city of Jerusalem where the temple was located. Some years earlier, the Jews evidently rebuilt most of the walls of Jerusalem (Ezra 4:6–23), but Nehemiah was distressed to hear that they had been broken down and the gates burned. Nehemiah responded by interceding for his people in their plight.

READING OF NEHEMIAH 1

Prayer:

Lord, You are the great and awesome God who hears the cries of Your people and grants us grace rather than retribution. I thank You that I can boldly approach the throne of grace to obtain mercy and find grace to help in time of need.

MEDITATION PASSAGE FOR TODAY:

verses 5–6, 10–11

N ehemiah served as the cupbearer to Artaxerxes king of Persia (464–423 B.C.). It was in the twentieth year of Artaxerxes (444 B.C.) that Nehemiah heard the disturbing news that the walls of Jerusalem had been reduced to a rubble. His sorrow was evident to the king; when Artaxerxes heard the cause of Nehemiah's concern, he invited him to make his request. Nehemiah was not caught unprepared and presented a clear plan of action to the king. He journeyed to Jerusalem with men and provisions, inspected the walls of the city, and encouraged its inhabitants to begin the good work of rebuilding. Nehemiah also refuted the accusations of the enemies of the children of Israel.

READING OF NEHEMIAH 2

Prayer:

Lord, I am grateful for the godly example of Nehemiah who had a passion for Your purposes and the plight of Your people. Give me a heart that seeks to be pleasing to You and the courage to set my hands to Your good work.

MEDITATION PASSAGE FOR TODAY:

verses 4, 18

U nder Nehemiah's leadership, the people of Jerusalem began the construction of the city wall with each group working in the area of their habitation. Seeing this, their enemies Sanballat and Tobiah sought to dishearten the people by mocking their efforts, but Nehemiah prayed and encouraged the people to continue. Alarmed at the progress of the work, their enemies plotted to attack and confuse the Jews, but Nehemiah prayed, put them in readiness, and encouraged them to continue. Half of the people worked while the other half continued the construction, and in this way they continued to progress without being intimidated by the threats of their enemies.

READING OF NEHEMIAH 4

Prayer:

Lord, I thank You for the balance of dependence and diligence illustrated in this chapter and for the godly leadership of Nehemiah who encouraged, exhorted, and equipped the people to continue the good work to which You called them. May I also press on in Your calling and stand firm in You in the spiritual warfare.

MEDITATION PASSAGE FOR TODAY:

verses 9, 14

Not only did the Jews experience external opposition from their enemies, but they were also suffering from internal oppression by their nobles and rulers. Hearing how many of the people were being forced into servitude through the financial exploitation of those who were exacting usury from their countrymen, Nehemiah rebuked these manipulators and required them to return the interest and stop abusing their brethren. Nehemiah also became an example to these nobles by refusing to take his rightful governor's provisions; instead, he shared with those who were in need.

READING OF NEHEMIAH 5

Prayer:

Lord, I know that opposition to Your calling in my life comes not only from without, but also from within. I ask that You would reveal any selfish and manipulative strategies that I have been guilty of following and set me free as I set my heart on Your Son.

MEDITATION PASSAGE FOR TODAY:

verses 9, 19

A s the work on the walls continued to progress, the enemies of the Jews continued to conspire to keep Jerusalem from being fortified. Sanballat, Tobiah, Geshem, and others sought to trick Nehemiah into leaving the work to meet with them so they could do him harm. Nehemiah wisely ignored their multiple messages and denied their false charges that he was fortifying the city to set himself up as king. Their next ploy was more subtle, since they hired Shemaiah to pose as a prophet of the Lord to get Nehemiah to hide himself in the temple. Nehemiah strengthened himself in the Lord and refused to succumb to intimidation. The walls were completed in only fifty-two days, evidence that the hand of God was upon them.

READING OF NEHEMIAH 6

Prayer:

Lord, thank You for the reminder that I too am engaged in a spiritual warfare between the forces of good and evil, and that I must be ever vigilant and dependent upon You. I will sanctify Christ as Lord in my heart and not be intimidated or fearful.

MEDITATION PASSAGE FOR TODAY:

verse 16

A fter the construction of the walls of Jerusalem, it was necessary to consecrate and consolidate the people. Just as Ezra the priest led reforms thirteen years earlier in Ezra 9–10 (457 B.C.), now he leads the children of Israel in a time of spiritual renewal as they recommit to their covenant with God (444 B.C.). Standing on a special platform that was built for the purpose, Ezra brought the Book of the Law, blessed the Lord, and read it to the congregation that gathered together to hear it. When the people heard God's Word, they wept in remorse, but Nehemiah the governor encouraged them to take strength in the joy of the Lord. The people responded to the Law by keeping the Feast of Booths for seven days as they continued to listen to the Book of the Law of God.

READING OF NEHEMIAH 8

Prayer:

Lord, I thank You for Your Word and for its ready availability. May I realize that the joy of the Lord is my strength and expose myself to Your truth each day with a heart to obey.

MEDITATION PASSAGE FOR TODAY:

verses 10–11

When the children of Israel gathered for a day of national fasting and penance, they heard a reading from the Book of the Law of the Lord and responded with a period of confession and worship. Their spiritual leaders guided them through a beautiful and powerful psalm of praise for the great deliverances of the Lord. This psalm recalls the work of God in creation, the calling and covenant with Abram, the deliverance of Israel from Egypt through the Red Sea, the giving of the Law on Mount Sinai, the rebellion of the people in the wilderness, the faithful provision of God, the conquest of the land, the kingdom, their unfaithfulness and consequent captivity, and a plea for restoration.

READING OF NEHEMIAH 9

Prayer:

Lord, You have always proven Yourself faithful to Your people in spite of our unfaithfulness and rebelliousness. May I remember Your many good works on my behalf and cling to You. Fill me with Your Holy Spirit so that I will walk in Your grace and power.

MEDITATION PASSAGE FOR TODAY:

verses 6, 17, 31

The Book of Esther takes place in 483–473 B.C. during the reign of Ahasuerus king of Persia (486–464 B.C.). Although the name of God does not appear in this book, His sovereign protection of His people who were scattered in the provinces of Persia is evident in its pages.

When Ahasuerus (known to the Greeks as Xerxes) made a feast for the many officials of the Medo-Persian Empire, he displayed his opulence and served wine in abundance. Queen Vashti also made a feast for the women. But when Ahasuerus sent for Vashti to come and display her beauty to the officials, she refused to obey. The king's counselors advised him to depose her to set an example throughout the empire that "every man should be the master in his own house."

READING OF ESTHER 1

Prayer:

Lord, I am reminded that the wealth and pomp of this world is fleeting and unsatisfying. Only those who find their identity and hope in You will enjoy true security, significance, and satisfaction.

MEDITATION PASSAGE FOR TODAY:

verse 4

When Ahasuerus' servants advised him to appoint officers throughout his kingdom who would search for beautiful virgins to gather to Susa, the king was pleased with the idea of selecting one of these women to replace his former queen. One of the women who was taken to the king's palace was Esther, a Jewish girl who had been raised by her relative Mordecai. While Esther was being prepared with the other virgins to see the king, she concealed her Jewish identity. When her turn came, this gracious and beautiful woman won the favor of Ahasuerus who had her crowned as his new queen.

Later, Mordecai warned Esther about a plot to assassinate the king, and she informed the king in Mordecai's name. The report was confirmed, the conspirators were hanged, and it was written in the court chronicles.

READING OF ESTHER 2

Prayer:

Lord, You sovereignly work in human affairs and use unknown and humble people to accomplish extraordinary things. Just as You chose this young woman to accomplish Your purposes, I ask that You would let me participate in Your purposes as well.

MEDITATION PASSAGE FOR TODAY:

verses 17, 20

A hasuerus' appointment of the arrogant Haman to the role of prime minister meant trouble for the Jews when Mordecai refused to bow or pay homage to him. When Haman heard of it and learned that Mordecai was a Jew, he plotted to destroy every Jew throughout the Persian Empire. He asked the king to allow him to draw up a royal decree to eliminate the Jews from every province on a day he had determined by casting Pur (the lot). When the decree was copied and sent by couriers throughout the many provinces of the empire, it caused consternation among all the Jewish people who heard of it.

READING OF ESTHER 3

Prayer:

Lord, the ugliness and destructive nature of human pride are evident in the rage and malice of Haman. I also realize that pride can cause me to react in ways that are utterly disproportionate to an offense, and I ask that You would protect me from the folly of self-promotion and arrogance.

MEDITATION PASSAGE FOR TODAY:

verse 4

When the Jews heard of the decree for their elimination, they cried out and mourned with fasting and sackcloth. Mordecai was among them, and when Esther heard he was wearing sackcloth, she sent Hathach, one of her attendants, to learn why Mordecai was mourning. He gave Hathach a copy of the decree and told him to request that the queen make intercession for her people. Esther responded that to go before the king uninvited would be to risk her life, but Mordecai sent word that her life would be forfeit with the rest of the Jews if she did not. Esther agreed to go to the king after the Jews in the city fasted three days for her.

READING OF ESTHER 4

Prayer:

Lord, You sovereignly orchestrate opportunities for Your people to participate in doing Your will on this earth. I ask that I would have the insight and courage to lay hold of the opportunities You bring so that I will not miss out on Your intentions for me.

MEDITATION PASSAGE FOR TODAY:

verses 13–14

After fasting for three days, Esther prepared to go before the king. When he saw her in the court, he favorably raised the golden scepter and invited her to approach. Asked to make a request, she invited the king and Haman to a private banquet. At the banquet, the king again invited her to make a request, so Esther asked them to come to another banquet on the following day where she would reveal her request. Haman was delighted with the apparent favor he was receiving and proudly recounted his position and privileges to his friends. When Haman said that all this was sullied by the disrespect of Mordecai, his wife suggested he have a gallows built and ask the king to have Mordecai hanged on it.

READING OF ESTHER 5

Prayer:

Lord, I thank You for the wisdom of Esther in contrast to the folly of Haman. In Your time and ways, the proud will be brought down and the humble will be raised up. May I seek the grace of humility and dependence upon You rather than the folly of arrogance and independence.

MEDITATION PASSAGE FOR TODAY:

verse 8

When the king providentially heard the account of Mordecai's averting an assassination attempt, he wanted him to be rewarded. Ironically, at that moment Haman was at court to ask the king to hang Mordecai. When the king asked Haman what should be done for the man the king wishes to honor, Haman proudly assumed the king meant him and answered accordingly. To his horror, Haman discovered the king intended this honor for Mordecai the Jew and that he should bring it about. When Haman told his wife and friends what happened, they realized he was about to fall before Mordecai. Just then, the king's eunuchs arrived to take Haman to Esther's banquet.

READING OF ESTHER 6

Prayer:

Lord, the rich irony and plot twists of this book display the truth of Mary's words in Luke 1: "He has scattered those who were proud in the thoughts of their heart. He has brought down rulers from their thrones, and has exalted those who were humble."

MEDITATION PASSAGE FOR TODAY:

verse 13

When the king and Haman went to Esther's second banquet, the king asked Esther to name her request. She then revealed her Jewish identity to the king and pled for the lives of her people. When the king asked who would presume to kill her and her people, the queen accused Haman of the deed. Haman was terrified. When the king went out in anger to the palace garden, Haman fell across Esther's couch, pleading for his life. When the king returned and saw this, the guard covered Haman's face. Then, at the suggestion of one of the eunuchs, the king ordered Haman to be hung on the very gallows he had prepared for Mordecai.

READING OF ESTHER 7

Prayer:

Lord, I thank You for this story about a woman who wisely discerned the fitting time and place to intercede on behalf of the Jewish people. May I also act in accordance with Your timing, Your way, and Your power.

MEDITATION PASSAGE FOR TODAY:

verse 3

Yet another irony in this book is the fact that Mordecai was given the house of Haman, the deceased enemy of the Jews. Esther sought to reverse the decree that Haman had deceitfully carried out in the name of the king. Since the former decree could not be revoked, the king granted Esther and Mordecai the right to issue another royal decree that would counteract the decree engineered by Haman. They acted quickly and arranged for the new decree to be carried throughout the provinces of the empire, which permitted the Jews to avenge themselves on those who would assault them. Because of this, "For the Jews there was light and gladness and joy and honor."

READING OF ESTHER 8

Prayer:

Lord, You hear the prayers of those who cry out to You and honor those who seek to honor You. In Your sovereignty, You even use the evil counsels of men to accomplish Your will, and nothing can thwart Your loving purposes for Your people.

MEDITATION PASSAGE FOR TODAY:

verse 16

O n the day appointed for the destruction of the Jews, the Jews throughout the provinces gathered and overpowered their enemies instead. Fear of them fell upon all the people, and they were able to defeat their adversaries. In the capital city of Shushan, the Jews killed five hundred enemies, including the ten sons of Haman. Esther requested that her people in Shushan be granted an additional day to defeat their opponents, and this was carried out. To commemorate their deliverance and victory, Mordecai and Esther decreed that the Jews celebrate an annual feast of Purim, named after Pur, the lot Haman had cast to fix the date for his decree to be enacted.

READING OF ESTHER 9

Prayer:

Lord, You are able to transform our sorrow into joy, and our travail into laughter. Thank You for this beautiful portrait of Your subtle but sovereign work. Help me remember the bigger picture of Your power and grace so I will abide in hope in times of adversity.

MEDITATION PASSAGE FOR TODAY:

verses 17, 22

The book of Job, evidently set around the time of the patriarch Abraham, teaches that God is sovereign over all things, and that He is worthy of our worship even when we do not understand what He is doing in our lives. Job was such a godly man that the Lord used him as an example to the Adversary, who promptly asserted that Job only worshiped God for His benefits, not for Himself. When God gave Satan permission to take away Job's material blessings, Job responded to the series of calamities by honoring God rather than charging the Lord with wrong.

READING OF JOB 1

Prayer:

Lord, I am amazed at the faith of Your servant Job who trusted You enough to hold fast to Your good character in spite of his devastating circumstances. Please give me the grace to depend upon You and trust You in all things, especially when I don't understand what is happening.

MEDITATION PASSAGE FOR TODAY:

verse 21

When Satan presented himself once again before the Lord, God affirmed Job's continued blamelessness in spite of Satan's heinous work of bringing disaster on Job's possessions and children. The Adversary pressed his previous claim that Job still served God because of His benefits, and pointed to Job's physical health. This time, the Lord allowed Satan to attack Job's person, but not to take his life. Satan immediately struck Job with painful boils all over his body, so that the pain was excruciating and unabated. Now reduced to nothing, Job still maintained his integrity and renounced his wife's advice to "Curse God and die!" When Job's three friends came to comfort him, they found him unrecognizable.

READING OF JOB 2

Prayer:

Lord, I can only wonder how I would respond under such adverse circumstances as these. Yet I know that other saints besides Job have endured as much and held fast to You. I ask for a heart of gratitude for Your many benefits and tender mercies, as well as a heart that loves You above all these.

MEDITATION PASSAGE FOR TODAY:

verse 10

The Book of Job records three cycles of debate between Job and his friends (first cycle: 3–14; second cycle: 15–21; third cycle: 22–26) that increase in emotional intensity as Eliphaz, Bildad, and Zophar claim that Job is suffering because of his sins while Job defends his innocence with growing vehemence. Job's responses, including his closing monologue (27–31) become increasingly self-righteous as he accuses God of not listening to him and of unjustly punishing him while allowing the wicked to prosper. Elihu finally speaks and urges Job to humble himself while God purifies him through the trials he is experiencing (32–37). The Lord Himself ends the debate by speaking to Job of his power and wisdom in creating and sustaining the world and all its creatures (38–39).

READING OF JOB 38

Prayer:

Lord, I realize that I am too nearsighted to understand what You are doing, and that I cannot read chapters 1–2 to glimpse the heavenly reasons for what is happening in my life. Let me understand that You are more concerned that I trust You than that I understand You, since Your ways exceed my own.

MEDITATION PASSAGE FOR TODAY:

verses 2–7

U sing a series of questions about the glories and wonders of His manifold and varied creation, the Lord teaches Job that God alone is in control of the created order. In chapters 38–39, the Lord refers to the earth, the sea, the sun, snow and hail, the wind and rain, the stars, lions, mountain goats, wild donkeys, the wild ox, the ostrich, the horse, the hawk, and the eagle. Each of these wonders reflects the handiwork of God and transcends human wisdom and power. Through these questions, the Lord reminds Job of his frailty and finitude and of his need to turn from his own wisdom to that of the omnipotent and infinite Lord of all creation.

READING OF JOB 39

Prayer:

Lord, when I reflect on the multitude of mysteries that surround me, I realize how foolish it is for me to question Your ways and doubt that You are in sovereign control. If You order the cosmos, I can surely trust You to order my life.

MEDITATION PASSAGE FOR TODAY:

verses 1, 5, 9, 19, 26–27

After the Lord's round of questions, Job responds by acknowledging his insignificance and presumption. He realizes that he has spoken about things of which he has no knowledge, and that his attempts to contend with the Almighty are borne out of foolishness. But the Lord wants Job to see more than this and, in a second speech to Job, illustrates His ability to control all things (40–41). The Lord tells Job that he would need to have the power of the Almighty to contend with Him and illustrates this power and authority in describing two of His many creatures. The first is the behemoth, a Hebrew word which appears only in Job 40:15. This awesome creature is only one of the manifold works of God.

READING OF JOB 40

Prayer:

Lord, I realize the presumption with which I grumble about my circumstances and indirectly accuse You of mismanagement. Thank You for this reminder that You alone are in sovereign control of all things, and that I cannot control even a day of my life.

MEDITATION PASSAGE FOR TODAY:

verses 6–14

After His poetic description of Behemoth, the Lord vividly describes another of His many creatures to illustrate His sovereignty over the entire created order and His ability to control the uncontrollable. As with Behemoth in Job 40, Leviathan in Job 41 is not easily identified. Judging from the poetic images of Leviathan's strength and size plus the other biblical passages that mention this creature, this appears to be a large sea creature. While it has been suggested that Behemoth is a hippopotamus and Leviathan is a crocodile, others think the descriptions in Job 40–41 seem to describe creatures that are larger and more powerful, even taking poetic exaggeration into account.

READING OF JOB 41

Prayer:

Lord, Your creation, with its rich array of extinct and existing animals and plants, abounds with marvels and wonders. Any one of these living things displays an elegance and complexity that greatly transcends our most advanced technology. May I always be more impressed by Your world than by the realm of human achievements.

MEDITATION PASSAGE FOR TODAY:

verses 1–5, 33–34

Job's response to God in 40:3–5 was a realization of his finitude and presumption, but here in 42:1–6 he responds in humility and repentance. His direct encounter with the awesome God of all creation brings him to the point of contrition for his self-righteousness that had been growing through the course of his debates with his friends as he sought to defend himself and questioned God's ways. The real issue in Job is not suffering, but sovereignty. The lesson Job ultimately learned through the things he suffered is that God alone is in sovereign control of all things. When Job prayed for his three friends, the Lord doubled what he had lost and gave him children to replace those He took away.

READING OF JOB 42

Prayer:

Lord, I am grateful that You care for Your people and teach us the painful lessons we need to receive. I see that You always intend good for us in the end, and that You are compassionate and merciful.

MEDITATION PASSAGE FOR TODAY:

verses 1–6

T he Psalter, comprising five books in one, powerfully and beautifully portrays the whole range of human emotions. Because of this, it has served as the most comforting and relevant book of the Bible for generations of believers. The psalms show us how to praise and worship God both in good and in difficult times, and they call us to put our hope in God and not in people or resources.

The first psalm is a fitting doorkeeper to the Psalter as a whole because of its stark contrast between the way of life and the way of death. It begins with a negative and positive description of the person who is blessed in the sight of God and sharply contrasts this with the fate of those who have rejected God's claims on their lives.

READING OF PSALM 1

Prayer:

Lord, I thank You for this clear reminder that those who delight in and meditate on Your instructions for living will grow and bear the fruit of character and joy. May I be responsive to Your Word and delight in it.

MEDITATION PASSAGE FOR TODAY:

verses 2–3

This psalm begins with a poetic description of God's general revelation in the world of nature (verses 1–6). Although we do not hear the sun and the stars, they speak with eloquence about the greatness and glory of God. The second part of the psalm is a hymn extolling the riches of the Lord's special revelation through His Word (verses 7–10). Six facets of the diamond of the Torah (law, testimony, precepts, commandment, fear, and judgments) refract the dazzling light of God's goodness and grace. The psalm concludes with a personal response to God's revelation in the world and the Word (verses 11–14). David expresses his intention to follow the way of God in his actions and attitudes.

READING OF PSALM 19

Prayer:

Lord, I marvel at Your greatness, glory, goodness, and grace. Your revelation in creation and in Your Word reveals Your glorious attributes and invites me to respond to Your loving overtures.

MEDITATION PASSAGE FOR TODAY:

verses 1, 7–11

The best known of all the psalms is a brief but marvelous meditation by a shepherd who draws an analogy between his caring relationship with his flock and the Lord's care for him. In the first two verses, David portrays the Lord as a shepherd who loves and cares for His flock. In the next two verses, the Lord is envisioned as a shepherd who guides and protects His sheep. The last two verses describe God as a shepherd who provides for and abides with His flock. This psalm poetically presents the ongoing goodness and mercy of the Lord throughout the life of His sheep.

READING OF PSALM 23

Prayer:

Lord, I thank You that I have become a member of Your flock through faith in Christ Jesus, and that Your presence will be my joy forever. May I become accustomed to practicing Your presence during the brief years of my earthly sojourn.

MEDITATION PASSAGE FOR TODAY:

verses 1–6

P salm 32, one of the seven "penitential psalms" (the others are Psalms 6, 38, 51, 102, 130, and 143), records the anguish and subsequent deliverance of a man who sought to deny and cover up his guilt before the holy eyes of God. The psalm opens with a joyful word about the blessing of forgiveness (verses 1–2); then in verses 3–5, David recalls the painful effects of his stubbornness and the turning point of his repentance. The wisdom of repentance is evident in the conclusion of the psalm. Those who do not know the Lord and believers who refuse to be honest with Him will try to cover up or rationalize their transgressions. Only when we turn to Him or turn back to Him can we know the liberation and blessing of forgiveness and newness of life.

READING OF PSALM 32

Prayer:

Lord, I thank You that You instruct me and teach me in the way I should go, and that mercy surrounds me when I trust in You. May I be glad in the Lord and rejoice in Your forgiveness.

MEDITATION PASSAGE FOR TODAY:

verses 1–2, 6–8

P salm 37 is a wisdom psalm that instructs us in the importance of maintaining the right perspective during our earthly journey. It is a beautifully crafted acrostic poem that begins almost every other verse with each successive letter of the Hebrew alphabet. Like the Book of Proverbs, this instructional poem contains wisdom sayings that encourage us to take the long view of life and see things from an eternal perspective. The bulk of this psalm contrasts the pursuits and destiny of the wicked and the righteous. It grants that in the short run, those who refuse to acknowledge God may prosper, while those who seek God often suffer at the hands of evildoers. But the righteous will ultimately endure and inherit the land.

READING OF PSALM 37

Prayer:

Lord, by Your grace I want to trust in You, to delight myself in You, to commit my way to You, and to be still and wait patiently for You. Thank You that I can rest in You and in this way overcome the concerns that would make me anxious.

MEDITATION PASSAGE FOR TODAY:

verses 3–7, 23–24, 39–40

P salm 73 is the record of Asaph's struggle with the issue of why good things happen to bad people and why bad things happen to good people. Asaph begins his meditation with an affirmation of the goodness of God, but honestly admits that he went through a crisis of faith in which he questioned the truth of this affirmation. Contrary to the prosperity gospel, there is no assurance that obedience to God will lead to material or physical well-being. When Asaph went to the temple to bring his affliction before the Lord, his perspective was radically changed. The turning point in the psalm is reached when the author takes his eyes away from the foolish pride of people and turns them to the glory and counsel of God.

READING OF PSALM 73

Prayer:

Lord, may I repent of the bitterness of heart that comes from putting my hope in anything other than Your goodness and promises. May I long for the things you declare to be important and live in the goodness of drawing near to You.

MEDITATION PASSAGE FOR TODAY:

verses 23–28

As "A prayer of Moses, the man of God" this is the oldest of the 150 psalms in the biblical Psalter. This thoughtful and poignant meditation on the brevity of human life was written almost 3,400 years ago, probably near the end of the wilderness wanderings of the children of Israel when Moses was in his final years. In spite of its antiquity, the message of this psalm speaks to our time with particular relevance and force. It begins with a brilliant contrast between the eternality of God and the brevity of human existence on earth, the pivotal verse asking the Lord to "teach us to number our days, that we may present to You a heart of wisdom" (verse 12). This psalm invites us to embrace an eternal perspective in a temporal world.

READING OF PSALM 90

Prayer:

Lord, I know that I cannot keep score by two systems. May I make the decision each day to be defined by the eternal so that I will not be defined by default by the temporal world system.

MEDITATION PASSAGE FOR TODAY:

verses 1–2, 12, 17

P salm 103, the first of a group of psalms of praise (Psalms 103–107), reminds us with skill and beauty that God's lovingkindness is the source of our greatest satisfaction. The psalm begins with a personal hymn of thanksgiving (verses 1–5) in which David recounts several reasons to praise the Lord from his personal experience of walking with Him. The psalm shifts in the second stanza from an individual thanksgiving to a communal hymn of praise around the theme of God's loyal love (verses 6–18). The third stanza of the psalm transports us from the individual and the community to the entire created order (verses 19–22). The meditation moves from God's grace to God's greatness as the psalmist invokes the myriad angelic and heavenly hosts to bless the holy Name.

READING OF PSALM 103

Prayer:

Lord, if I do not love You with my whole being, I will love some lesser good with my whole being. I ask that I would put You first in my affections and seek You as my supreme good and final joy.

MEDITATION PASSAGE FOR TODAY:

verses 1–5, 8, 11–13

This beautiful hymn of praise explores the entire created order as a testimony to the glory of God and His wonderful works on every level from the great to the small. It begins with the majesty of God Himself and journeys from the heavens to the earth. The psalmist considers the large-scale features of the earth's atmosphere, oceans, and land masses, and focuses in on the rich variety of creatures that inhabit this planet, including wild donkeys, birds, vegetation, trees, wild goats, rock badgers, lions, and sea creatures. Everything comes from the hand of the Lord, and it is He who sustains all living systems. When God's people meditate on the creation, they renew their appreciation for His greatness and glory.

READING OF PSALM 104

Prayer:

Lord, may Your glory endure forever, and may You be glad in Your works. May my meditation be pleasing to You, and may I be glad in the Lord and rejoice in all You have done.

MEDITATION PASSAGE FOR TODAY:

verses 1–2, 24, 31

P salm 107 is a resource that encourages us to keep a grateful memory alive by remembering God's benefits in the past. The psalmist creates four different scenes to depict the return of the Israelites from Babylonian captivity and uses the same refrain of thanksgiving near the end of each: "Let them give thanks to the LORD for His lovingkindness, and for His wonders to the sons of men!" All four scenes reveal the folly of thinking we are masters of our fate. We would be wise to recognize ourselves in the fourfold picture of plight and salvation: *we* are the wanderers, the prisoners, the sick, and the storm-tossed who have been retrieved, released, restored, and rescued.

READING OF PSALM 107

Prayer:

Lord, I know that in Your severe mercy You sometimes take me to the end of my rope, but You are always faithful to those who cling to You during the tough times of life. May I cultivate an ongoing attitude of gratitude by remembering the good things You have done for me.

MEDITATION PASSAGE FOR TODAY:

verses 1, 8, 43

There is no higher calling than to love and worship the infinite and personal God of creation and redemption. In complete contrast to the world, God's economy measures greatness not in terms of ability or accomplishments, but in the vitality and integrity of a person's walk with the Lord. This meditation on the Person and works of God reveals the depth of David's relationship with God. Its four stanzas are reflections on the attributes of God: God is all-knowing (verses 1–6), all-present (verses 7–12), all-powerful (verses 13–18), and all-holy (verses 19–24). God knows us intimately and is present with us in any adversity we face.

READING OF PSALM 139

Prayer:

Lord, I ask with David that You would search me, and know my heart; try me, and know my anxious thoughts; and see if there be any hurtful way in me, and lead me in the everlasting way.

MEDITATION PASSAGE FOR TODAY:

verses 1–3, 14, 23–24

The last of the Davidic psalms exhorts us to fly with the wings of the Spirit to the pinnacle from which we can see everything from a biblical viewpoint. Psalm 145, a skillfully constructed acrostic poem, invites the people of God to let their spirits resonate with His Spirit as it alternates calls to praise and reasons for praise. It begins with the unsearchable greatness of God (verses 1–8) and the glorious splendor of His majesty. The psalm then moves to the theme of the goodness of God (verses 9–13) and His tender mercies that are over all His works. David concludes with a meditation on the grace of God (verses 14–21) and the way He fulfills the desire of those who call upon Him and fear Him.

READING OF PSALM 145

Prayer:

Lord, I will extol You, my God, O King, and I will bless Your name forever and ever. You are great and highly to be praised, and Your greatness is unsearchable. All Your works shall give thanks to You, O Lord, and Your godly ones shall bless You.

MEDITATION PASSAGE FOR TODAY:

verses 1–3, 5, 8, 17–21

DAY 156—PROVERBS 1

P roverbs is an immensely practical and specific book that challenges us to pursue wisdom in each area of everyday life. It counsels us to depend upon and order our ways before God in our relationships with our wives or husbands, children, work, friends, and neighbors. It also encourages us to develop a godly character that will become evident in our speech, our use of money and time, and the decisions we make.

The purpose of Proverbs is expressly given in 1:2–6. This book was collected first to impart moral insight and astuteness (1:2a, 3–5), and second to help the reader develop mental ability and understanding (1:2b, 6). The theme of this book is captured in verse 7: "The fear of the LORD is the beginning of knowledge; fools despise wisdom and instruction."

READING OF PROVERBS 1

Prayer:

Lord, may I respond to wisdom's call and avoid the enticement of folly. I want to receive the instruction of wisdom, justice, judgment, and equity so that I will walk in prudence and discernment.

MEDITATION PASSAGE FOR TODAY:

verses 2–7

DAY 157—PROVERBS 2

The book of Proverbs begins by preparing the reader to receive instruction (1–9). A clear statement of the purpose of the book (1:1–7) is followed by a series of ten exhortations as from a father to a son that are designed to encourage the student to treasure and pursue the priceless gem of wisdom. The benefits of wisdom are manifold, since they lead to true success and character in life as opposed to the pain and destruction that result from a life of folly. The discipline of wisdom leads to freedom and skillful living, whereas the path of foolishness and rebellion makes a person vulnerable to the lures and seductions of the lusts of this world. In this chapter, we are encouraged to seek diligently for wisdom because of her many benefits.

READING OF PROVERBS 2

Prayer:

Lord, I want to treasure Your words and incline my ear to wisdom. I know that You are the source of wisdom, and that You are a shield to those who fear You and walk in Your ways.

MEDITATION PASSAGE FOR TODAY:

verses 1–9

The word translated "wisdom" (*hokhmah*) relates to the idea of skill (it was used of Bezalel and Oholiab, the skillful men who fabricated the tabernacle). This book stresses that it is through instruction, discipline, and practice that we learn the skill of living our lives in such a way that they amount to something excellent and worthwhile. When we fear the Lord by developing a sense of awe, humility, and dependence upon Him, God refines us and shapes us into the people He wants us to become, much as a skilled artist takes raw materials and transforms them into a beautiful work. Wisdom is derived from whole-hearted trust in the Lord rather than ourselves. The opposite of wisdom is the folly of arrogance and autonomy.

READING OF PROVERBS 3

Prayer:

Lord, may I trust in You with all my heart and not lean on my own understanding. In all my ways I want to acknowledge You, so that You will make my paths straight.

MEDITATION PASSAGE FOR TODAY:

verses 5–7

The family was intended to be the relational context in which children are encouraged and instructed in the development of character, virtue, knowledge, and wisdom. One of the central messages in these nine chapters that introduce the maxims beginning in chapter 10 is that we can learn and live, not just live and learn. These are principles and precepts that have been hammered out long before us, so we do well to build upon this foundation of received knowledge and insight instead of reinventing the wheel ourselves. Each generation has the responsibility to impart these truths to the next.

READING OF PROVERBS 4

Prayer:

Lord, may I watch over my heart with all diligence, for from it flow the springs of life. May I put away from me a deceitful mouth and put devious speech far from me. May I look directly ahead and watch the path of my feet.

MEDITATION PASSAGE FOR TODAY:

verses 7, 23–27

The exhortations of Proverbs are both positive and negative, stressing both the benefits of wisdom and the destructive effects of foolishness. In this chapter, the son is warned about the subtle deceits of the immoral woman. These exhortations are preventive; they anticipate issues and temptations the child will face in the future. If we have not thought out our convictions in advance, they will not be there to serve us at the point of temptation and action. These verses counsel us to remain faithful to the spouse we have been given, and warn us about the dangerous lures of infidelity and adultery.

READING OF PROVERBS 5

Prayer:

Lord, may I remember that my ways are ever before You, and that You watch all my paths. Keep me from the snares of iniquity, and let me walk in fidelity to the relationships You have given me.

MEDITATION PASSAGE FOR TODAY:

verses 1–2, 21

P roverbs 6 is a little collection of practical counsel in various areas of life. It warns us against financial commitments that can ensnare us down the road and of the folly of risking more money than we can afford to lose. It warns us about the trap of slothfulness and self-indulgence, and it counsels us to avoid those who stir up slander, strife, and discord among people. It also exhorts us to avoid the devastating consequences of immorality and adultery. All these instructions are designed to get us to think before we act. Those who sin in haste will unfortunately have plenty of time for sorrow and repentance.

READING OF PROVERBS 6

Prayer:

Lord, may I carefully listen to these words of strong counsel concerning money, sloth, self-indulgence, slander, discord, pride, deceitfulness, and immorality.

MEDITATION PASSAGE FOR TODAY:

verses 20–23

P roverbs 7 and 8 contrast folly and wisdom by personify-
ing them as two radically different women. The woman
of folly is portrayed as a seductress who flatters the naïve with
her words and who presents herself not only in open places, but
also in dark corners. She can be subtle and persuasive, seducing
by appeals to pride and rationalization. Her speech is enticing
and persistent, and those who are lured into the trap of folly
never think about the disastrous consequences of the way that
leads to death.

READING OF PROVERBS 7

Prayer:

*Lord, may I keep Your words and treasure Your commands
within me. The lures and entrapments of the way of folly are
ever present, and I know that yielding to the seductions of money, sex, and power would draw me away from You.*

MEDITATION PASSAGE FOR TODAY:

verses 1–5

The beautiful personification of wisdom as a woman in chapter 8 is a portrait of the perfection of righteousness and morality (verses 8–9). This wisdom is divine (verses 22–31), the wellspring of all biological and spiritual life (3:18; 8:35–36). Proverbs stresses that wisdom is not limited to an elite class of people but is accessible to all who are willing to seek it. As the New Testament teaches, Christ Jesus is the incarnation of wisdom: He "became to us wisdom from God, and righteousness and sanctification, and redemption" (1 Corinthians 1:30). In Christ "are hidden all the treasures of wisdom and knowledge" (Colossians 2:3).

READING OF PROVERBS 8

Prayer:

Lord, may I listen to Your instruction and be wise enough to respond to Your exhortations and find life by seeking Your favor. Let me love You and Your ways, and thus avoid the ways of death.

MEDITATION PASSAGE FOR TODAY:

verses 32–36

The proverbs themselves do not begin until chapter 10. In this last preparatory chapter, wisdom is personified as a virtuous woman who invites those who lack understanding to come to her well-provisioned table.

These pithy sayings of Solomon and others cover a wide variety of issues, though for the most part, they are not arranged in any topical manner. The Hebrew word *mashal* "proverb" means a comparison or a similitude, and the proverbs use figures of speech to make comparisons and penetrating insights. The proverbs, based upon careful observations of accumulated experience, were designed to be easily committed to memory and are simple illustrations that expose fundamental realities about life.

READING OF PROVERBS 9

Prayer:

Lord, thank You for Your gracious invitation to receive the abundance of life and blessings You offer. I affirm that the fear of the Lord is the beginning of wisdom, and the knowledge of the Holy One is understanding.

MEDITATION PASSAGE FOR TODAY:

verse 10

Proverbs concludes with a number of precepts and comparisons by Agur (30) and Lemuel (31), ending with an acrostic poem depicting a wife of noble character in verses 10–31. This portrait of a wise woman is a timeless and ever-relevant model for women. She is intelligent, creative, industrious, prudent, and discerning. She plans carefully and makes informed decisions that benefit others. She manages her household with diligence and grace, and she looks to the Lord as her source of strength.

READING OF PROVERBS 31

Prayer:

Lord, thank You for this portrait of the woman of virtue, dignity, diligence, and grace. I thank You that in every time and culture, these principles can be applied by those who seek You first.

MEDITATION PASSAGE FOR TODAY:

verses 30–31

DAY 166—ECCLESIASTES 3

T he need for satisfaction and significance in life drives most people to pursue these things in the wrong places — in the created order rather than the Creator of order. Ecclesiastes, written by a king (evidently Solomon) whose abilities, assets, and attainments are far beyond our own, is a road map that shows us where the human quest apart from God ends up. It is a warning, by a person who had it all, that the world will never satisfy our deepest longings, since these can only be satisfied in a relationship with the living God. This is because we have been created in His image; thus He has "set eternity in [our] heart" (3:11).

READING OF ECCLESIASTES 3

Prayer:

Lord, You have made everything appropriate in its time. You have also set eternity in our heart, yet so that no one can find out the work which You have done from the beginning even to the end.

MEDITATION PASSAGE FOR TODAY:

verses 1, 11

DAY 167—ECCLESIASTES 12

E cclesiastes was written at the end of an unprecedented pursuit of wisdom, power, pleasure, possessions, and accomplishments, and it uses this experience to demonstrate that none of these things can fill the empty void in the human heart. It was Augustine who said that God created us for Himself, that our hearts are restless until they find their rest in Him. Ecclesiastes is a commentary on this truth, developing the theme that the search for the highest good must not be limited to that which is "under the sun" (this expression appears 29 times) but must end in the fear and obedience of God (12:13).

READING OF ECCLESIASTES 12

Prayer:

Lord, I know that apart from You life is empty, meaningless, and futile; that it is characterized by inequity, injustice, and uncertainty. But with You, there is hope, meaning, and reason for rejoicing.

MEDITATION PASSAGE FOR TODAY:

verses 1, 13–14

This beautiful homage to the love that germinates and blossoms between a man and a woman stood out among the 1,005 songs written by Solomon (1 Kings 4:32) as "the Song of Songs." It is a literary masterpiece of oriental symbolism, layered metaphors, and rich imagery that eulogizes the glories of romantic love. This song is intimate, but it never sinks to vulgarity in its portrayal of attraction, desire, pleasure, consummation, separation, companionship, and growth in the relationship between lovers. The physical and emotional aspects of marital love are a gift from God designed to be enjoyed in an other-centered way.

READING OF SONG OF SOLOMON 1

Prayer:

Lord, this poetic portrait of love between a man and a woman also points beyond itself, by way of application, to the intimate relationship You invite us to have with You. I ask for the grace of increased passion for You.

MEDITATION PASSAGE FOR TODAY:

verse 4

I saiah has been called "the Shakespeare of the prophets" and "the Mt. Everest of Hebrew prophecy" for good reasons. This comprehensive and superbly written book is the high water mark of Messianic prophecy which can be regarded as the Bible in miniature. The first 39 chapters loosely correspond to the 39 books of the Old Testament in their condemnation of sin and emphasis on judgment, while the last 27 chapters loosely correspond to the 27 books of the New Testament in their message of consolation and hope.

Chapter 6 presents a vision of the majesty of the living God and the commissioning of Isaiah to a prophetic mission to God's rebellious people.

READING OF ISAIAH 6

Prayer:

Lord, You are awesome in holiness, and the whole earth is full of Your glory. I thank You that You are concerned for the welfare of Your people and that You want us to find life, blessing, and hope in You.

MEDITATION PASSAGE FOR TODAY:

verses 1–5

DAY 170—ISAIAH 40

T his beautiful chapter dramatically introduces the prophecies of comfort that conclude the Book of Isaiah. It is with sorrow that Isaiah announces in the first 39 chapters that the kingdom of Judah will go into captivity because of her continual rebellion against the Lord. But chapters 40–66 proclaim a glorious message of future hope and blessings for the people of God.

Isaiah 40 opens with a word of comfort and anticipation of God's personal deliverance and grace for those who look to Him. With magnificent poetic imagery, the wisdom, sovereignty, majesty, and perfect ways of God are unfolded.

READING OF ISAIAH 40

Prayer:

Lord, I thank You for Your lovingkindness, Your infinite wisdom, Your limitless power, Your wonderful beauty, and Your authority over all things. I take comfort in Your changeless character, and I wait upon You alone.

MEDITATION PASSAGE FOR TODAY:

verses 11, 25–26, 31

I saiah is the most comprehensive of the Old Testament prophets and offers the clearest portrait of the coming Messiah. Isaiah has rightly been called the "Saint Paul of the Old Testament" because of his systematic exposition, his clarity and power, his sweeping scope, and his striking imagery. He is quoted in the New Testament more than any other prophet, with about 85 allusions to chapter 53 alone.

This text presents five aspects of the saving work of Messiah: (1) His sacrifice was wholehearted (burnt offering; 52:13-15), (2) His character was perfect (meal offering; 53:1-3), (3) He brought atonement that issues in peace with God (peace offering; 53:4-6), (4) He paid for the transgression of the people (sin offering; 53:7-9), and (5) He died for the effects of sin (trespass offering; 53:10-12).

READING OF ISAIAH 53

Prayer:

Lord, I give thanks for this clear portrait of the saving work of Christ that was written seven centuries before His crucifixion. Thank You that He suffered sinlessly, silently, and as a substitute for us.

MEDITATION PASSAGE FOR TODAY:

verses 3-7, 12

The prophetic condemnation (1–39) is followed by a prophetic consolation (40–66) in which the Lord comforts His people with a message of hope and restoration. The sovereignty and majesty of God is the foundation for Israel's hope (40–48). He alone rules the realms of nature and of nations; His power and greatness are contrasted with the impotence of idols. The salvation of God centers on the redemptive work of the coming Servant who will save His people from their iniquities (49–57).

In this chapter, Messiah invites everyone to come and find life in Him. Those who seek the Lord will be satisfied with His righteousness.

READING OF ISAIAH 55

Prayer:

Lord, I will seek You while You may be found, and call upon You while You are near. I forsake evil and return to You, and I thank You that You have compassion on me and abundantly pardon.

MEDITATION PASSAGE FOR TODAY:

verses 1, 6–11

I n chapters 58–66, the restoration of God will extend to all who have come to Him in humility and trust, and Messiah Himself will reign over the earth in His glorious kingdom.

Jesus the Messiah quoted verses 1–2a in the synagogue in Nazareth (Luke 4:18–19), telling His hearers that these words were fulfilled in Him. It is significant that He stopped before the words, "and the day of vengeance of our God," since this concerns His second advent. The Lord loves justice, and will bring an everlasting kingdom of righteousness, rejoicing, and praise upon the earth.

READING OF ISAIAH 61

Prayer:

Lord, I will rejoice greatly in You, and my soul will exult in my God. For You have clothed me with garments of salvation, and have wrapped me with a robe of righteousness.

MEDITATION PASSAGE FOR TODAY:

verses 1–2, 8, 10

J eremiah was called to the unenviable prophetic ministry of urging a rebellious people to repentance for nearly five decades without any significant positive response. Instead, he experienced public humiliation, was put in stocks, was forced to flee for his life, was thrown into a cistern, and was misunderstood by virtually all who encountered him. In spite of his frequent discouragement and pain, he remained faithful to his calling and endured to the end. He is a striking model of faithfulness and steadfast endurance in the face of opposition.

The sign of the potter in Jeremiah 18 is an object lesson that illustrates the opportunity God gives His people to repent before they are judged, and their stubborn refusal to do so.

READING OF JEREMIAH 18

Prayer:

Lord, I do not want to walk according to my own plans or follow the vain imaginations of my heart. May I be responsive to Your call and return to You when I stray from Your ways.

MEDITATION PASSAGE FOR TODAY:

verses 6, 11–12

The sign of the potter's earthenware jar is another illustration to the people of Judah of the irrevocable consequences of their apostasy, idolatry, and immorality. Jeremiah took some of the elders of the people and priests to the Valley of Hinnom near the potsherd gate of Jerusalem and proclaimed a prophetic word of condemnation due to the spiritual infidelity of the people. Then Jeremiah shattered the jar in their sight to portray the way God would break the people and the city. This scene summarizes the prophetic burden of this whole book: in spite of God's covenant love for His people, they have corrupted themselves through spiritual harlotry and are beyond the point of repentance.

READING OF JEREMIAH 19

Prayer:

Lord, I know Your character is perfect and uncompromisingly holy and that my own thoughts, words, and deeds have separated me from You. But I thank You that I have been restored to peace and union with You through the gift of faith in the righteousness of Christ.

MEDITATION PASSAGE FOR TODAY:

verse 15

Jeremiah's prophecy about the coming new covenant anticipates the new covenant that was inaugurated through the
blood of Christ (Matthew 26:26–29). In spite of the prophetic
condemnation of Judah because of the people's sin and rebellion, there is also a prophetic consolation because of God's mercy and grace. In verses 31–34, the Lord proclaims that He will
make a new covenant with Israel and Judah in which He will
implant His righteousness in their hearts and take away their
iniquity. Unlike the Mosaic covenant which was external and
could not be fulfilled by human effort or merit, the new covenant is internal and is fulfilled by God's indwelling Spirit.

READING OF JEREMIAH 31

Prayer:

*Lord, I thank You that You inaugurated the new covenant
through the blood of Your Son, and that You have made me
a beneficiary of this covenant through faith in His completed
work. Thank You that Christ now dwells in me, and I in Him.*

MEDITATION PASSAGE FOR TODAY:

verses 3, 31–34

The sad and mournful set of five elegiac poems known as Lamentations is striking in its emotional content, its beauty, and its literary structure. Writing with a broken heart, Jeremiah identifies with the sorrow of his people and the apparent destruction of their future, but he pauses to remember the faithfulness and lovingkindness of his God. It is a reminder to us to hold fast to God's character, especially in the distressing times of life.

In the third lament, Jeremiah empathizes with the anguish and despondency of his people but also finds hope when he considers the compassion and faithfulness of the Lord.

READING OF LAMENTATIONS 3

Prayer:

Lord, Your lovingkindnesses indeed never cease, for Your compassions never fail. They are new every morning; great is Your faithfulness. "The Lord is my portion," says my soul, "Therefore I have hope in Him."

MEDITATION PASSAGE FOR TODAY:

verses 22–26

E zekiel is an extraordinary book of mystery, visions, symbolism, parables, and allegories that stretches our minds about the glory and majestic splendor of God, inviting us to fear Him and hope in Him. This is a complex and multifaceted collection of prophetic oracles which offers a number of significant keys to grasping God's future program to bring salvation and righteousness upon the earth.

Ezekiel's vision of the glory of God in chapter 1 is one of the most remarkable passages in Scripture, and it is the first of a series of passages that trace the localized manifestation of the presence of God's glory from its departure from the temple to its return to the new temple (1:28; 3:12, 23; 9:3; 10:4, 18–19; 11:22–23; 43:1–5; 44:4).

READING OF EZEKIEL 1

Prayer:

Lord, I marvel at Your awesome being, majesty, and holiness. The appearance of the likeness of the glory of the Lord in this chapter transcends my comprehension and causes me to realize how little I really know about You.

MEDITATION PASSAGE FOR TODAY:

verses 4, 22, 26–28

After Ezekiel was divinely commissioned to be a prophet to the Jewish exiles in Babylon (2–3), he delivered a series of prophetic condemnations that focused first on Judah (4–24), then on the surrounding nations (25–32). The final section of Ezekiel's prophecy (33–48) was delivered after Jerusalem's destruction and turns from the theme of condemnation to a message of consolation. God's judgment came just as He promised; His promise of the future blessing, gathering, and restoration of Israel will just as surely be fulfilled. The dramatic vision of the reanimation of the dry bones anticipates the restoration and purification of Israel and Judah. The book then concludes with details of the new temple, the new Jerusalem, and the new land (40–48).

READING OF EZEKIEL 37

Prayer:

Lord, I thank You that You are faithful to Your covenant promises in spite of the unfaithfulness of Your people. I am grateful for this vision of restoration, renewal, and the reign of the coming King.

MEDITATION PASSAGE FOR TODAY:

verses 3–6, 12–14, 26–28

D aniel is an extraordinary book because of its sweeping overview of the rise and fall of the kingdoms of men, its anticipation of the kingdom ruled by Messiah that will never fall, and the character of the prophet himself. Daniel's remarkable life from his teenage years to the time of his old age illustrates a variety of biblical principles that are relevant to our lives as people who live in a culture that is hostile to spiritual growth and commitment.

Daniel's personal background and preparation is presented in chapter 1. Daniel and his friends remain faithful to the Lord and refuse to compromise their convictions during the time of their training for service in Babylon.

READING OF DANIEL 1

Prayer:

Lord, the example of this faithful and godly figure challenges me to honor You and avoid areas of compromise in my life. May I walk before You in dependence upon the indwelling righteousness of Christ.

MEDITATION PASSAGE FOR TODAY:

verses 8–9

I n chapters 2–7, the language switches from Hebrew to Aramaic, since this portion of the book outlines God's sovereign plan for the Gentiles. The visions and interpretations in this section reveal how God will raise up and overthrow four Gentile empires, after which He will establish an everlasting kingdom.

The dream of Nebuchadnezzar in chapter 2 illustrates the primary theme of this book; the power and dominion of God over human affairs. The God of Israel has authority over all nations. It is He who changes the times and the epochs; He removes kings and establishes kings; He gives wisdom to wise men and knowledge to men of understanding (2:20–22).

READING OF DANIEL 2

Prayer:

Lord, You have authority over all history and over all the kingdoms of this world. I am grateful for the sure hope that these temporal kingdoms will be replaced by Your everlasting kingdom through the sovereign reign of the Lord Jesus.

MEDITATION PASSAGE FOR TODAY:

verses 20–22

S eeing himself as the head of gold in his dream in Daniel 2, Nebuchadnezzar erects a golden image and demands that all bow to it. Having been appointed to positions of authority, this image provides an occasion for the enemies of Daniel's friends to accuse them of disloyalty to the king because of their refusal to worship it. When they respectfully decline the king's urging to bow to the image, Nebuchadnezzar is furious and orders that they be burned alive in a superheated furnace. The king is stunned when he sees them walking unharmed in the fire accompanied by an awesome being. The persecution and preservation of Daniel's friends illustrates the power of God to protect His people in times of tribulation.

READING OF DANIEL 3

Prayer:

Lord, the example of these men who trusted You regardless of the outcome reminds me of my need to depend completely on Your character both in smooth and in troubled times. May I honor You by putting no conditions on my trust.

MEDITATION PASSAGE FOR TODAY:

verses 17–18, 28

Nebuchadnezzar was alarmed by a night vision of a great tree that was reduced to a stump, so he called Daniel to interpret the dream when his diviners could not. Daniel was appalled by the meaning of the vision but faithfully related it to the king, urging him to avert the disaster by turning from his iniquities and showing mercy to the poor. The king was too proud to heed this wise counsel, and the Lord fulfilled the vision by reducing him to an animal-like state for seven years. At the end of this time, the Lord restored Nebuchadnezzar's reason and reestablished his kingdom. The now-humbled king gave honor to the Most High God who "does according to His will in the host of heaven and among the inhabitants of earth."

READING OF DANIEL 4

Prayer:

Lord, I know that You, the Most High, are ruler over the realm of mankind, and that You bestow it on whom You wish. Deliver me from the folly of pride when things appear to go my way, and let me walk in wisdom, fearing Your holy name.

MEDITATION PASSAGE FOR TODAY:

verses 17, 25, 34–35

After his long reign over Babylon (605–562 B.C.), Nebuchadnezzar was succeeded by three kings with brief reigns, and then by his son-in-law Nabonidus (556–539 B.C.). Because he was constantly fighting the Medes and Persians, Nabonidus arranged a coregency with his son Belshazzar (553–539 B.C.). In his last feast, Belshazzar defied the God of Israel by using gold vessels from the former temple in Jerusalem. When a hand appeared and wrote on the palace wall, the terrified king sought an interpreter: Daniel was summoned out of obscurity. The prophet rebuked the king for his pride and predicted the overthrow of Babylon in his interpretation of the writing. That night the Persians diverted the water of the Euphrates, went under the gates, and took over the city.

READING OF DANIEL 5

Prayer:

Lord, I know that those who exalt themselves against the Lord of heaven will be cast down. May I humble myself before You and glorify Your name and not my own.

MEDITATION PASSAGE FOR TODAY:

verse 21–23

During the reign of Darius the Mede (his relationship to Cyrus king of Persia [559–530 B.C.] mentioned in Daniel 10:1 is not clear), Daniel so distinguished himself that the commissioners and satraps saw him as a threat. To overthrow Daniel, they manipulated Darius to sign a document forbidding anyone to make a petition to anyone but him for thirty days on pain of death. Knowing Daniel's habit of praying three times a day, they accused him of violating the injunction. Darius was trapped by his own edict and forced to condemn Daniel to the lions' den. The next morning, the king was delighted to find that God had delivered Daniel (who was over 80 years old at this point) and issued a decree honoring the God of Daniel.

READING OF DANIEL 6

Prayer:

Lord, I thank You for the character, conviction, and faithfulness of Your servant Daniel who never lost sight of who is in control and walked steadily with You in spite of fluctuating circumstances. May I also live a life that demands an explanation by walking with You throughout the years of my earthly sojourn.

MEDITATION PASSAGE FOR TODAY:

verses 5, 16, 22–23

I n chapters 8–12, the language switches from Aramaic back to Hebrew, since this section overviews God's prophetic plan for Israel. These chapters describe Israel under the Medo-Persian and Grecian empires. They also detail the coming kings of Persia and Greece, the wars between the Ptolemies of Egypt and the Seleucids of Syria, and the persecution under Antiochus Epiphanes in the second century B.C. The people of God will be delivered from tribulation and raised from the dead (12).

Chapter 9 records the third of Daniel's four visions. After his prayer of confession on behalf of his people, God's faithful servant was given the revelation of the seventy weeks which gives the chronology of God's plan for the redemption and deliverance of His people, predicting the time of Messiah's atoning death.

READING OF DANIEL 9

Prayer:

Lord, Your Word clarifies my present experience by giving me perspective on Your plan and purposes. You are the great and awesome God, who keeps Your covenant and lovingkindness for those who love You and keep Your commandments.

MEDITATION PASSAGE FOR TODAY:

verses 4–5, 24–27

H osea ("salvation") was a prophet to the northern king-dom of Israel (often named Ephraim after its largest tribe; 5:3–13) in the days of its last six kings. Hosea's lengthy time of service (from about 755 B.C. to about 710 B.C.) made him a contemporary of Isaiah and Micah, as well as a younger contemporary of Amos, who also prophesied to the northern kingdom.

Hosea's personal affliction (1–3) illustrates Israel's coming national catastrophe (4–14). After bearing him three children, Gomer abandons Hosea and becomes an adulteress. When she is reduced to slavery, Hosea publicly redeems her and restores her. In the same way, Israel has committed spiritual adultery through corruption, injustice, and willful idolatry, and resolute-ly refusing to repent (4–7).

READING OF HOSEA 4

Prayer:

Lord, I ask that I will not succumb to pride by taking Your gifts and benefits for granted. When I sin against You, give me a humble willingness to repent and yield the control of my life to You.

MEDITATION PASSAGE FOR TODAY:

verses 1, 6, 10

DAY 188—HOSEA 14

B ecause of Israel's hardness of heart, she will be brought into a judgment of dispersion and destruction (8–10). God's holiness and justice require Him to discipline Israel, but because of His steadfast love and compassion, He will restore Israel in the future (11–14).

The book of Hosea offers a profound illustration of the way we are loved by God. His love for us is unconditional, but it is also marked by His holiness. Because of this, God seeks better things for us than the things we choose for ourselves. This book reminds us of our need to turn back to the Lover of our souls whenever we have strayed from Him.

READING OF HOSEA 14

Prayer:

Lord, I know that Your ways are right, that the righteous will walk in them, but transgressors will stumble in them. I thank You that when I stumble, I can return to You and receive Your cleansing grace.

MEDITATION PASSAGE FOR TODAY:

verses 1–2, 4, 9

J oel's theme is the day of the Lord that will come upon Judah and the nations. He uses Judah's dreadful experience of a recent locust plague to illustrate the devastation that awaits the nation if they do not humbly turn to the Lord in repentance and obedience. The day of judgment upon Judah is seen in terms of a coming locust plague, and the Lord appeals through His prophet to "return to Me with all your heart, and with fasting, weeping and mourning" (2:12). Images of disaster are prominent in this book, including not only locust plagues, but also famine, fires, invading armies, and phenomena in the heavens. After their judgment is completed, the people of Judah and all who call on the name of the Lord will be saved (2:32).

READING OF JOEL 2

Prayer:

Lord, when I stray, may I always return to You, for You are gracious and compassionate, slow to anger and abounding in lovingkindness.

MEDITATION PASSAGE FOR TODAY:

verses 12–13, 25, 27–32

A lthough Amos lived in Judah (Tekoa was 12 miles south of Jerusalem), he was sent by God as a prophet to the northern kingdom of Israel. "I am not a prophet, nor am I the son of a prophet; for I am a herdsman and grower of sycamore figs. But the LORD took me from following the flock and the LORD said to me, 'Go, prophesy to My people Israel'" (7:14–15).

Amos, like James in the New Testament, does not mince his words, but delivers a series of sharp and incisive declarations and images that arouse the conscience and require a response. This book is relevant to our times because it was addressed to a materialistic culture that fostered greed, injustice, and arrogance. It is a word of warning that such a culture cannot continue for long without being diminished by divine judgment.

READING OF AMOS 1

Prayer:

Lord, I serve an awesome and holy God, and I must order my steps before You in repentance and righteousness. May I make a difference in my time by expressing Your righteousness in the way I live and relate to others.

MEDITATION PASSAGE FOR TODAY:

verse 2

The book of Amos begins with a series of eight prophetic oracles that pronounce judgment on the nations that surround Israel (1–2). The word "fire," a symbol of judgment, often appears in this section, and, as a map will show, the sequence of the seven nations gradually spirals in on the last nation, Israel. This "funnel of fire" demonstrates the iniquities of these countries, and that judgment is unavoidable. In three sermons, each beginning with the phrase, "Hear this word" (3:1; 4:1; 5:1), Amos outlines the reasons for Israel's coming overthrow. In spite of all that God has done, He tells them, "yet you have not returned to Me" (4:6, 8–11). Because of their refusal to turn to Him, He will send them into exile beyond Damascus (5:27).

READING OF AMOS 2

Prayer:

Lord, may I listen responsively to Your Word with a heart to obey Your exhortations and walk in Your truth.

MEDITATION PASSAGE FOR TODAY:

verses 4, 6

I n a series of five visions (7:1–9:10), Amos pictures the coming judgment on the northern kingdom of Israel. Because of Amos' intercession, the first two judgments of locusts and fire will not take place. In the vision of the plumb line, Israel is like a leaning wall; in the vision of the basket of ripe fruit, Israel is rotten and overripe for judgment.

Amos is an extraordinarily concise and penetrating prophet who multiplies oracles and images to hammer home the solemn theme of inescapable judgment. Only in the last five verses is there a message of hope and promise. The three promises at the end of the book (9:11–15) are that God will restore the line of David, rebuild the nation, and renew the people.

READING OF AMOS 9

Prayer:

Lord, You are faithful to keep Your promises in spite of our unfaithfulness. May I order my steps before You and walk in hope.

MEDITATION PASSAGE FOR TODAY:

verses 5–6, 13–15

With only 21 verses, Obadiah is the shortest book in the Old Testament, and yet it is a complete message with the twin prophetic themes of condemnation (1–16) and consolation (17–21; the consolation portion concerns Judah, not Edom). The burden of Obadiah is a pronouncement of inescapable doom upon the Edomites (Esau) because they looked down on their brother Judah (Jacob) in the day of his misfortune and rejoiced over the people of Judah in the day of their disaster (12–14). The Edomites' pride will be brought low (3–4), and they will be ransacked (6), terrified (9), and obliterated (10). Israel, on the other hand, will be restored and will possess its inheritance (17–21).

READING OF OBADIAH

Prayer:

Lord, I realize that the things we do to other people eventually come back to us, and that we can either sow to please the flesh and reap corruption, or we can sow to please the Spirit and reap blessing.

MEDITATION PASSAGE FOR TODAY:

verses 3–4, 15, 17

E verything in Jonah (the storm, the lots, the sailors, the great fish, the people of Nineveh, the vine, the worm, and the east wind) obeyed God's command except for the prophet himself. God told Jonah to go northeast to Nineveh; instead, he got on a boat that was heading west to Tarshish (possibly Spain). He knew that if he preached a message of repentance to the Assyrians, they might respond, and this would make him feel like a traitor to his own people. God's purpose would not be thwarted, however, so He sovereignly prepared a great fish to deliver the disobedient prophet and to change his perspective.

READING OF JONAH 1

Prayer:

Lord, I know that disobedience to Your calling creates pain and confusion in my life. But I also know that my failures do not disqualify me from Your service as long as I am willing to repent and return to You.

MEDITATION PASSAGE FOR TODAY:

verses 9, 16–17

J onah's prayer of praise to God for delivering him from a watery grave is followed by a divine recommissioning to preach to the people of Nineveh. God prepares a "great fish" (the text does not say "whale") to preserve Jonah and deliver him on dry land. The fish and its divinely appointed rendezvous with the sinking prophet became a powerful reminder to Jonah of the sovereignty of God in every circumstance.

Jonah's experience of being engulfed by the deep, engorged by a great fish, and later deposited alive on land is used by Christ as a type of His death, burial and resurrection (Matthew 12:39–40).

READING OF JONAH 2

Prayer:

Lord, there is no limit to what You can use to get my attention when You teach and test me. I thank You for Your deliverances and I affirm that salvation is from the Lord.

MEDITATION PASSAGE FOR TODAY:

verses 7, 9

J onah obeys God's second commission to go to Nineveh when he becomes "a sign to the Ninevites" (Luke 11:30). (The prophet would have been a walking object lesson from God if his skin was bleached from hours in the stomach of the fish.) As he moves through the city, his one-sentence sermon evokes a remarkable response of repentance and fasting among the people of Nineveh. Because of His great mercy, God "relented concerning the calamity which He had declared He would bring upon them."

Thus, Jesus declared, "The men of Nineveh will stand up with this generation at the judgment, and will condemn it because they repented at the preaching of Jonah; and behold, something greater than Jonah is here" (Matthew 12:41).

READING OF JONAH 3

Prayer:

Lord, I am grateful that You are gracious and compassionate, slow to anger and abundant in lovingkindness, and one who relents concerning calamity.

MEDITATION PASSAGE FOR TODAY:

verses 9–10

When the Ninevites respond with repentance and fasting, Jonah reacts with anger rather than rejoicing, because he resents God's willingness to show mercy to his enemies. The Lord teaches Jonah a lesson on compassion by using a vine as an object lesson.

We typically want God to treat us with grace and to treat our enemies with justice. Jonah is the story of a man who resisted God's call to prophesy to the capital city of Israel's archenemy, Assyria. He was afraid that if he prophesied to the people of Nineveh, they would repent and God would avert the disaster that was due to come in 40 days. This little book teaches us about the folly of resenting the grace of God when it is extended to people we think should not receive it. We can be thankful that God's mercy moves beyond national borders.

READING OF JONAH 4

Prayer:

Lord, Your intentions extend beyond our personal borders since You are the ruler not only of nature, but also of all nations. May I never allow my personal bias to stand between me and Your purposes.

MEDITATION PASSAGE FOR TODAY:

verses 2, 10–11

T he prophecy of Micah opens with a declaration of coming judgment upon the northern kingdom of Israel (Samaria) and the southern kingdom of Judah (Jerusalem). The cause of this judgment is listed as premeditated crime, covetousness, fraud, and lying prophets (1:1–2:11). Nevertheless, there is a word of hope in God's promises of regathering and deliverance (2:12–13).

Micah next focuses his prophetic barbs on the ungodly rulers and false prophets of Israel and Judah and predicts a coming disaster upon them (3). This word of condemnation is followed by a consoling announcement of future restoration through the reinstitution of the kingdom under the rule of Messiah (4–5).

READING OF MICAH 5

Prayer:

Lord, I am grateful for Your promise that You will do what people in all ages have failed to do — bring in a kingdom of universal peace, justice, and righteousness.

MEDITATION PASSAGE FOR TODAY:

verses 2, 4

In the concluding section of this book (6–7), God calls the people into court and summons the whole earth to witness against them (6:1–2; cf. 1:2). In spite of God's acts of gracious deliverances, His people have rejected Him and walked in dishonesty, injustice, and treachery. But the book closes with a series of promises that God will restore the remnant and pardon their transgressions (7:7–20).

Micah's particular concern is with the social sins of exploitation and injustice. The problem of political corruption, greed and arrogance among religious leaders, and false prophets who were more interested in personal gain than in corporate goodness permeated the kingdoms of Israel and Judah. As the prophet of the poor and the downtrodden, Micah has particular relevance to the conditions we face in our own culture.

READING OF MICAH 7

Prayer:

Lord, may I do justice, love kindness, and walk humbly before You. You are the God who pardons iniquity and delights in unchanging love.

MEDITATION PASSAGE FOR TODAY:

verses 7, 18–20

N ahum's prophecy opens with a description of Yahweh's righteous character. He is "a jealous and avenging God" who "takes vengeance on His adversaries" (1:2). His power is unlimited, and no one can endure His anger (1:3–6). Those who trust in Him discover His goodness and grace, but He overcomes His foes (1:7–8). Because of His holiness, He condemns the wickedness of Nineveh (1:9–14) and comforts those who are righteous in Judah (1:15).

Using vivid imagery, Nahum describes the siege and the plundering of Nineveh after the invading warriors move through the breach in its wall (2). As the chariots and charging cavalry invade, the city is thrown into chaos, and there is no one to mourn for it (3:1–7). Just as the Assyrians overthrew Thebes, Egypt's proud capital, so Assyria's capital will also be destroyed in spite of its many fortifications (3:8–18). Because of Assyria's cruelty, everyone will rejoice at its fall (3:19).

READING OF NAHUM 1

Prayer:

Lord, You are good, a stronghold in the day of trouble, and You know those who take refuge in You. May I never presume on Your grace but trust wholly in You.

MEDITATION PASSAGE FOR TODAY:

verses 2–3, 7, 15

When Habakkuk saw the growing wickedness in his countrymen as they shamelessly disobeyed the laws of God and openly distorted justice on every level, he wondered how God could allow this to go on without bring Judah to judgment. God's answer to his question was that He was raising up the Babylonians as His rod of judgment on Judah, but this answer only increased Habakkuk's confusion. The Babylonians were even more violent and depraved than the people of Judah—how could God allow this? God's second answer helped him better understand the goodness, perfection, wisdom, and power of Yahweh. With a clearer grasp of the *Person* of the Lord, he had a greater capacity to trust the *purposes* of the Lord. Thus, Habakkuk could conclude his book with confidence rather than complaint, with praise rather than perplexity.

READING OF HABAKKUK 3

Prayer:

Lord, I want to live by faith and by hope in You, especially in times when the circumstances surrounding me make me question whether You are in control and know what You are doing.

MEDITATION PASSAGE FOR TODAY:

verses 17–19

L ike the majority of Old Testament prophets, Zephaniah develops the twin themes of condemnation (1:1–3:8) and consolation (3:9–20). The bulk of the book concerns the primary theme of judgment; like Joel before him, Zephaniah's central image of judgment is "the day of the Lord." This image appears 23 times in different forms in this short book of three chapters, refering to a judgment that is universal (1:2–3; 3:8), imminent (1:14), and wrathful (1:15–17). But there is another side of the day of the Lord that points to restoration (3:9–13) and blessing (3:14–20).

Zephaniah is a powerful and condensed book that uses vivid and gripping imagery to communicate an unrelenting message about the day of judgment that would not only come to Judah and the nations that surrounded Judah, but will also come in the future to all the nations of the earth.

READING OF ZEPHANIAH 3

Prayer:

Lord, I thank You that You exult over Your loved ones with joy, that You are quiet in Your love, and that You rejoice over Your people with shouts of joy.

MEDITATION PASSAGE FOR TODAY:

verses 5, 9, 15, 17

This brief prophecy was delivered to a people whose spiritual lives were in decline because they had allowed their priorities to become misplaced. In a series of sharp exhortations, Haggai encouraged them to consider their ways, to take action, and to take heart. This little book provides a strong word to us when we find ourselves discouraged and despondent because of spiritual lethargy.

In his first sermon to the Jewish remnant, Haggai told them that they needed to reorder their priorities. Because they were more concerned with their own comfort than with their spiritual well-being, God was withholding His material blessing. Zerubbabel the governor of Judah, Joshua the high priest, and the whole remnant responded to Haggai's message, by resuming construction on the temple (1:1–15).

READING OF HAGGAI 1

Prayer:

Lord, I thank You for this lesson that when we value the spiritual above the material in our lives, You take care of our material needs. But when we value the material above the spiritual, we not only miss out on the spiritual, we are never satisfied with the material.

MEDITATION PASSAGE FOR TODAY:

verses 12–13

H aggai's second sermon was a word of encouragement that in spite of the small scale of the second temple, its glory would be greater than that of the former temple, and it would be a place of peace (2:1–9). The third message of this book is addressed to the priests and concerns purification from the contamination of sin and the need for obedience (2:10–19). The final oracle reaffirms God's plan to overthrow the nations of the earth (2:20–23; cf. 2:6–7).

Haggai called the Jewish remnant to the realization that God actually increased their hardships to get their attention, and to cause them to look to Him rather than themselves for the meeting of their needs. If they seek Him first and honor Him by finishing the temple, God will bless them and provide for their material needs.

READING OF HAGGAI 2

Prayer:

Lord, may I look to You and not my work as the source of my provision, knowing that You use my work as a means, but You are the source. I know that when I forget this, I will be tempted to put my security in money by planning according to income rather than according to priorities.

MEDITATION PASSAGE FOR TODAY:

verses 4–9

The visions and exhortations of Zechariah 1–8 were given to the prophet in Jerusalem during the rebuilding of the temple by the returned remnant. The purpose of this portion of the book, dated from November of 520 B.C. to December of 518 B.C., was to encourage the people to complete the new central sanctuary and to help them realize that it was not simply a building but a key to their spiritual identity. The Messiah would appear in this very temple when He came to bring salvation to His people.

Zechariah evidently received the two oracles of chapters 9–14 a few decades after the completion of the temple in 516 B.C., and they are directly concerned with the coming Messiah and Israel's restoration after the time of the Gentiles. These oracles were given to comfort and reassure the remnant that despite the uncertainties and hardships they were encountering, the Lord regathered them for a purpose and has a glorious future for them in the Messianic kingdom.

READING OF ZECHARIAH 14

Prayer:

Lord, am grateful for this promise of Messiah's coming to be king over all the earth. Come quickly, Lord Jesus!

MEDITATION PASSAGE FOR TODAY:

verses 3–5, 9

M alachi delivers this oracle as a dialogue between God and His people in which the Lord seeks to penetrate the barriers that the priests and people have erected between themselves and their God. The religious and moral corruption of the people reveal a condition of spiritual lethargy marked by an attitude that it does not pay to serve the Lord. They have convinced themselves that in spite of their religious observances, God has not alleviated their difficult circumstances. But the Lord tells them that their lack of blessing is not due to divine indifference but to their hypocrisy, lack of sincerity, and disobedience to His moral law. When they repent and return to God, God will return to them (3:7) and bless their labors.

READING OF MALACHI 3

Prayer:

Lord, I know that my religious observances become stale and meaningless when they are not accompanied by a wholehearted desire to honor and trust You.

MEDITATION PASSAGE FOR TODAY:

verses 1–3, 6–7

Malachi anticipates the coming of the Lord's messenger who will prepare the way for the Messiah. "Behold, I am going to send My messenger, and he will clear the way before Me. . . . Behold, I am going to send you Elijah the prophet before the coming of the great and terrible day of the LORD" (3:1; 4:5; cf. Isaiah 40:3). One aspect of this prophecy was fulfilled by John the Baptist who typified the coming of Elijah before the day of the Lord (Matthew 3:3; 11:10–14; 17:9–13; Mark 1:2–3; 9:10–13; Luke 1:17; 3:4–6; John 1:23). But another aspect awaits the appearance of Elijah himself before the second advent of Christ (3:2–3). The last of the Old Testament prophets anticipates the coming of the first of the New Testament prophets, John the Baptist, but there would be a 400–year prophetic silence between them.

READING OF MALACHI 4

Prayer:

Lord, I thank You that for those who fear Your name, the sun of righteousness will rise with healing in its wings. Your name, O Lord, will be great among the nations.

MEDITATION PASSAGE FOR TODAY:

verse 2

Matthew is the first of the five historical books (the Gospels and Acts) that make up 60 percent of the New Testament. These books lay the foundation upon which the epistles are built, showing how the life of Christ and the acts of the apostles are embedded in a historical context. The gospel of Matthew stresses the lordship of Christ and His perfect fulfillment of many Old Testament Messianic passages. It is a portrait of Jesus that invites us to respond in humility and obedience to His loving authority.

Matthew begins his account of the presentation and rejection of Israel's Messiah and King by unveiling the credentials of Jesus as the direct descendant of David, the King of the Jews sought by the Magi, the fulfillment of John the Baptist's preaching, and the sinless One who overcame the satanic temptations in the wilderness (1–4). In His matchless Sermon on the Mount (5–7), Jesus teaches that God looks on the heart and not merely our actions.

READING OF MATTHEW 5

Prayer:

Lord, may I let my light shine before others in such a way that they may see my good works, and glorify my Father who is in heaven.

MEDITATION PASSAGE FOR TODAY:

verses 3–10, 16–18

The four gospels are not biographies but thematic portraits of Jesus Christ that are addressed to particular audiences and stress distinct aspects of the life of Christ. These unique portraits combine together to create a composite picture in which the total is greater than the sum of the parts.

In Matthew 6, Jesus tells His listeners that when they give, pray, and fast, they should do these things to please God rather than impress people. In His model prayer and in His teaching on anxiety, Jesus stresses the need to focus first on the Father and to look to Him for every good thing.

READING OF MATTHEW 6

Prayer:

Lord, hallowed be Your name. Your kingdom come, Your will be done, on earth as it is in heaven. May I store up treasures in heaven by seeking first Your kingdom and righteousness.

MEDITATION PASSAGE FOR TODAY:

verses 9–13, 20–21, 24, 33–34

I n this last portion of His Sermon on the Mount, Jesus exhorts us to examine ourselves when we are tempted to have a censorious attitude toward others. He invites us to ask, seek, and knock so that we will receive the things we need from our Father in the heavenlies. He encapsulates the Law and the Prophets in His commandment to treat people the same way we want them to treat us.

Jesus brings this sermon to a climax when He urges his listeners not merely to hear, but to act upon His words. Only by entrusting ourselves to Him will we be founded on the rock.

READING OF MATTHEW 7

Prayer:

Lord, grant me the grace to seek You, to enter through the narrow gate, and to build my house upon the rock of Christ.

MEDITATION PASSAGE FOR TODAY:

verses 1, 7–8, 12

The Sermon on the Mount is followed by a collection of miracles that reveal Jesus' authority over nature, disease, demons, and death. Thus, His words are authenticated by His works (8–10). As the people hear Jesus' words and see His works, the religious leaders begin to oppose Him, as this theme of mounting rejection is developed until it culminates in the crucifixion. In response to this opposition, Jesus begins to speak in parables and spends more time with His disciples to prepare them in light of His coming death and resurrection (11–20).

In Matthew 13, Jesus uses parables to conceal the truth from those who would reject it, and to reveal the truth to those to whom it was granted to receive the mysteries of the kingdom of heaven.

READING OF MATTHEW 13

Prayer:

Lord, Your kingdom is like a treasure hidden in the field and like a pearl of great value. May I give everything I have in exchange for Your kingdom and righteousness.

MEDITATION PASSAGE FOR TODAY:

verses 11–12, 44–46

Matthew builds a solid case that Jesus fulfills the qualifications for Israel's Messiah in His lineage, His healing ministry, and His teachings. He does this by using more Old Testament quotations and allusions than any other New Testament book (almost 130). The expression, "what was spoken through the prophet was fulfilled," recurs nine times in this gospel but does not appear in the other three gospels. This is a book of fulfillment in which Jesus as the Christ or Messiah uniquely fulfills the Messianic prophecies of the Hebrew Bible and offers Himself to Israel as her King. This is seen in the phrase, "the kingdom of heaven," which appears 32 times in Matthew and nowhere else in the New Testament. This is an important theme, because the Jewish reader would wonder why Jesus did not overthrow the Romans and establish the promised kingdom if He was indeed Israel's Messiah.

READING OF MATTHEW 17

Prayer:

Lord, You veiled Your preincarnate glory and humbled Yourself in Your incarnation, Your servant ministry, and Your redemptive death. I rejoice that the story does not end there but continues with Your glorious resurrection, Your ascension, Your second coming, and Your eternal kingdom.

MEDITATION PASSAGE FOR TODAY:

verses 5, 22–23

M ore than any of the other gospels, Matthew emphasizes the Jewish background of the life of Christ and assumes its readers have a detailed knowledge of the Hebrew Bible and of Jewish customs and religious traditions. Matthew also stresses the teachings of Jesus: 60 percent of its 1,071 verses contain His spoken words. These include two of the three major discourses of our Lord, the Sermon on the Mount (5–7) and the Olivet Discourse (24–25); the third is the Upper Room Discourse in John 13–17. This gospel is highly structured with thematically arranged sections that present Jesus' miracles, parables, questions, and discourses. It converges on the central theme of mounting opposition by the religious leaders to the Person of Jesus. Their rejection of His offer leads to the climax of the book in His death, burial, and resurrection.

READING OF MATTHEW 21

Prayer:

Lord, may I consider Him who has endured such hostility by sinners against Himself, so that I will not grow weary and lose heart. I give thanks that You loved us so much that You sent Your Son, and I am grateful for His loving obedience to Your will.

MEDITATION PASSAGE FOR TODAY:

verses 5, 9, 21–22

After His triumphal entry into Jerusalem, Jesus primarily addresses those who have rejected their rightful King. He predicts the downfall of the city and the dispersion of the Jewish people among the nations, as well as the events associated with His second coming as Judge and Lord (21–25). The gospel culminates in the crucifixion, the supreme act of rejection (26–27), and the resurrection, God's supreme act of vindication and exaltation (28).

In the first part of the Olivet Discourse, Jesus anticipates the destruction of Jerusalem that would later take place in A.D. 70, looks beyond this to speak of an unprecedented time of tribulation, and exhorts all to be ready for His second advent.

READING OF MATTHEW 24

Prayer:

Lord, heaven and earth will pass away, but Your words will not pass away. May I heed Your words and live in readiness as I anticipate Your coming.

MEDITATION PASSAGE FOR TODAY:

verses 14, 21–24, 35

The Olivet Discourse continues with two parables that illustrate the judgment of Israel and the need to be on the alert in view of the certain coming of the King. Those like the foolish virgins who only professed to be ready to meet the bridegroom will not enter the kingdom, and those like the slave who buried the talent that was given him will be excluded from the joy of their master.

When the King comes and sits upon the glorious throne of David, all the nations will be gathered before Him, and He will judge the people of the earth. The sheep are those who receive the gospel and serve Jesus by serving His people, and the goats are those who reject the gospel of the kingdom.

READING OF MATTHEW 25

Prayer:

Lord, may I serve You by serving the people You love. By Your grace, may I hear Your words, "Well done, good and faithful slave. You were faithful with a few things, I will put you in charge of many things; enter into the joy of your master."

MEDITATION PASSAGE FOR TODAY:

verses 13, 21, 31, 40

M atthew 26–27 portrays the betrayal, arrest, trial, and crucifixion of Israel's rejected King. Once again Jesus predicts His crucifixion, and the chief priests and elders plot together to kill Him. The anointing of His head by Mary of Bethany and His betrayal by Judas anticipate His impending death which takes place at the time of the Jewish Passover, thus linking the Messianic Son of Man with the Paschal lamb. At the Lord's supper, Jesus connects His death to the new covenant and predicts that His disciples will leave Him. After the agony of Gethsemane, the Lord is betrayed by Judas, abandoned by His disciples, denied by Peter, and brought before Caiaphas and the Sanhedrin where He is accused of blasphemy for claiming to be the Son of God.

READING OF MATTHEW 26

Prayer:

Lord, I am amazed at the vastness of Your love that endured rejection by Your people, betrayal and abandonment by Your disciples, and the agony of anticipating the awful burden of taking the cumulative sins of the world upon Yourself.

MEDITATION PASSAGE FOR TODAY:

verses 26–29

The combined gospel accounts reveal that Jesus endured six trials. The first three were religious (before Annas, Caiaphas, and the Sanhedrin), and the last three were civil (before Pilate, Herod, and again before Pilate). When Judas realized the outcome of the deliberations, he threw the blood money into the temple and later hanged himself. Jesus was brought before Pilate, then after his encounter with Jesus, the governor was unsuccessful in his attempt to release Him. After handing Him over, Jesus was scourged, mocked, spat upon, and beaten by the Roman soldiers and then led to the place of crucifixion outside the city walls. After the pain and humiliation of the crucifixion, Jesus yielded up His spirit, and was buried in Joseph of Arimathea's tomb.

READING OF MATTHEW 27

Prayer:

Lord, it is impossible for me to grasp the fullness of this mystery, that the eternal Son of God would endure such rejection, humiliation, sorrow, and agony to reconcile sinful people to You. I thank You for the new covenant with You that was purchased through His blood.

MEDITATION PASSAGE FOR TODAY:

verses 46, 54

This glorious account of the empty tomb, the resurrection, and the appearances of Jesus to His disciples authenticates His words and works and demonstrates that Jesus Christ is indeed the prophesied Messiah and King. The tomb had been sealed and guarded, but the angel of the Lord rolled away the stone and told the women who had come to the tomb that it was empty. They encountered the resurrected Lord on their way to tell the disciples that He had risen from the dead, and Jesus told them to have the disciples leave for Galilee where they would see Him. The guards went to the Jewish elders and were paid to say that the disciples stole the body. When the disciples later saw Jesus in Galilee, He gave them the Great Commission to make disciples of the nations.

READING OF MATTHEW 28

Prayer:

Lord, all authority has been given to Your Son in heaven and on earth. May I be actively involved in His Great Commission to proclaim the good news to others and help others grow in His grace.

MEDITATION PASSAGE FOR TODAY:

verses 18–20

The Gospel of Mark is the most clear and concise of the four gospels, using a quick-paced narrative style to tell the story of the suffering Servant who constantly engaged in other-centered ministry through healing, teaching, and preaching. This is a book that stresses the power of servanthood and the reality of finding our life by losing it for Christ's sake, just as He gave His life for our sake. Like the other gospels, Mark disproportionately emphasizes the final week of the earthly life of Christ with 40 percent of its material dedicated to the last eight days.

Chapters 1–4 emphasize the words of the Son of God, while chapters 5–7 focus more on His works. In chapter 6, Jesus teaches at Nazareth, sends out the twelve, feeds the multitude, walks on the water, and heals the sick wherever He encounters them.

READING OF MARK 6

Prayer:

Lord, You identified with us in our humanity through the humility and servanthood of the incarnation. I give thanks for this and for the way You also demonstrated Your complete authority over nature, disease, demons, and death.

MEDITATION PASSAGE FOR TODAY:

verses 4, 31, 34, 51–52, 56

L ike the other gospels, Mark is not a biography but a thematic narrative that approaches the life of Christ from a specific
perspective. The theme of this gospel is evident in Christ's clear
purpose statement in 10:45: "For even the Son of Man did not
come to be served, but to serve, and to give His life a ransom
for many." The eighteen miracles in Mark demonstrate not only
the compassion of the Lord but also His power and authority,
and they authenticate His teachings which are interspersed
throughout.

Jesus responds to mounting opposition by intensifying His
teaching and preparation of His disciples so that they will be
prepared for His departure. In the period between 8:27 and
10:52 (approximately six months), Jesus tells His disciples of
His coming death and resurrection with increasing frequency
as He turns His steps to Jerusalem.

READING OF MARK 8

Prayer:

*Lord, may I be willing to come after Jesus by denying myself,
taking up my cross, and following Him. May I find life by losing it for Your sake and the gospel's.*

MEDITATION PASSAGE FOR TODAY:

verses 2, 27–29, 34–38

L uke is the most comprehensive of the Gospels, marked by careful chronological development and accurate historical details. It combines with Acts as the first of a lengthy two-part historical narrative that begins with the foretelling of the birth of John the Baptist and ends with Paul's first Roman imprisonment. Luke is a beautifully written gospel that documents the perfect humanity of Jesus and presents Him as the Son of Man who seeks us out and makes it possible for us to have a life-giving relationship with Him.

Luke places a strong emphasis on the ancestry, birth, and early years of the perfect man and of His forerunner John the Baptist. Their infancy stories are intertwined as Luke records their birth announcements, advents, and temple presentations.

READING OF LUKE 1

Prayer:

Lord, I delight in Mary's response to Gabriel's announcement, "Behold, the bondslave of the Lord; may it be done according to your word." I ask for the grace to respond to Your perfect will in humility, trust, and obedience.

MEDITATION PASSAGE FOR TODAY:

verses 17, 30–38, 42–55, 76–79

Day 222—Luke 2

N ot only is Luke the longest of the four gospels, but it is also the longest book in the New Testament. When this gospel is combined with Acts, it constitutes 28 percent of the New Testament. Luke is also the most historically detailed of the Gospels, and its refined literary Greek is rivaled only by Hebrews in the New Testament. Luke's extensive vocabulary and wide range of expressions enhance this book. The four hymns in chapters 1 and 2 have added immensely to Christian worship (these are the *Magnificat* of Mary in 1:46–55, the *Benedictus* of Zechariah in 1:67–79, the *Gloria in Excelsis* of the heavenly host in 2:14, and the *Nunc Dimittis* of Simeon in 2:28–32).

READING OF LUKE 2

Prayer:

Lord, I thank You for the good news of great joy in Christ the Lord, our Savior, Redeemer, Advocate, and King.

MEDITATION PASSAGE FOR TODAY:

verses 10–14, 29–32, 52

J esus prepared over thirty years (summarized in 2:52) for a public ministry of only three years. After the infancy narratives and summary of the ministry of Jesus' forerunner John the Baptist, the ancestry of the Son of Man is traced back to the first man Adam. Just before Jesus launches His public ministry, He is baptized by John and led into the wilderness by the Holy Spirit where He encounters the powerful temptations of Satan. Like the first Adam, the last Adam is tempted by the lust of the flesh, the lust of the eyes, and the boastful pride of life (1 John 2:16), but unlike the first Adam, our Lord resists the devil. Early in His ministry He is rejected by the people of His hometown Nazareth. Beginning in Capernaum, Jesus demonstrates His authority over the realms of demons, disease, nature, and human traditions (4:31–6:49).

READING OF LUKE 4

Prayer:

Lord, I am grateful for Jesus' willingness to endure temptation, rejection, spiritual warfare, and physical weariness in order to accomplish His purpose of preaching the kingdom of God.

MEDITATION PASSAGE FOR TODAY:

verses 32, 36, 41, 43

A s Jesus progresses in His ministry of preaching, healing, and demonic expulsion, He encounters the dual response of growing belief and growing rejection. In this and the following chapters, Luke places particular stress on the perfect humanity as well as the kindness and compassion of Jesus. His concern for all classes and conditions of people (poor and wealthy, women, Jews, Samaritans, Gentiles, tax collectors, and religious leaders) is especially evident in this book. Luke portrays Christ's solidarity with the human condition in His identification with the sorrowful and sinful plight of people. In 9:51 Jesus commences His last journey to Jerusalem, and in light of mounting opposition, He prepares His disciples for His departure by teaching and building His life into them.

READING OF LUKE 7

Prayer:

Lord, I marvel at the compassion, gentleness, and grace of Your Son who healed the blind, the lame, the lepers, and the deaf; who raised up the dead; who preached good news to the poor; and who offered forgiveness to sinners.

MEDITATION PASSAGE FOR TODAY:

verses 22, 47–50

This remarkable chapter presents three parables that illustrate the same theme. The parables of the lost sheep, the lost coin, and the lost son are Jesus' response to the criticism of the Pharisees and the scribes that He receives sinners and eats with them. In each story, something valuable is lost, an effort is made to find it, and there is rejoicing and celebration when it is restored. These stories point to the joy in heaven when one sinner repents and turns to God. The parable of the prodigal son reveals an especially poignant description of God as a loving father who waits for his wayward child to return. Seeing his son in the distance, he runs after him, embraces him, and kisses him.

READING OF LUKE 15

Prayer:

Lord, when I was lost and dead in my trespasses and sins, You sought me and found me. I treasure Your embrace and know that I am only at home when I am with You.

MEDITATION PASSAGE FOR TODAY:

verses 7, 10, 20, 24, 32

The parable of the unrighteous steward is a surprising illustration of the fact that the children of this world are more shrewd in relation to their own kind than the children of light. This story teaches us to leverage the temporal assets of time, talent, and treasure to build into people, since relationships centered on others are the currency of heaven. Jesus calls us to treat things according to their true value by pursuing the things He declares to be important. The story of the rich man and Lazarus also illustrates the need to live our lives in light of eternity instead of giving ourselves in exchange for that which is passing away.

READING OF LUKE 16

Prayer:

Lord, I know that the things that are highly esteemed among men are detestable in Your sight. May I devote myself to You as Your servant and turn away from the folly of chasing after earthly wealth.

MEDITATION PASSAGE FOR TODAY:

verses 8–10, 13, 15, 31

Day 227—Luke 18

As He continues on His final journey to Jerusalem, Jesus instructs His disciples on a number of practical matters including covetousness, readiness, repentance, the kingdom of God, salvation, evangelism, discipleship, forgiveness, faithfulness, humility, gratitude, the second coming, prayer, and wealth. Jesus encourages His disciples to be diligent and persistent in their prayers. He contrasts the futility of works righteousness with the need to approach God in a humble and childlike manner. And He assures His disciples that they will be disproportionately rewarded for whatever they have given up for His sake.

READING OF LUKE 18

Prayer:

Lord, may I never put my trust in my own efforts to attain righteousness or view other people with contempt. I ask for a spirit of humility that looks to Your grace instead of my own achievements.

MEDITATION PASSAGE FOR TODAY:

verses 1, 14, 16–17, 29–30

As the Lord enters Jericho on His way to Jerusalem, He transforms the life of a wealthy tax collector by giving Zaccheus the gift of salvation. Jesus encapsulates His ministry purpose in His declaration that "the Son of Man has come to seek and to save that which was lost." The parable of the minas illustrates the truth that reward in the kingdom of God is not determined by what we have been given, but by faithfulness in how we use what God has entrusted to us.

In His triumphal entry into Jerusalem, Jesus presented Himself as Israel's promised Messiah. Seeing the city, He wept over it, knowing that it would be destroyed because of Israel's rejection of her King who had come in the name of the Lord.

READING OF LUKE 19

Prayer:

Lord, I desire to be faithful with all that You have given to me, knowing that I will one day give an account to You.

MEDITATION PASSAGE FOR TODAY:

verses 10, 26, 38, 42

After cleansing the temple by driving out those who were exploiting it for financial gain, the Lord encountered the opposition of the chief priests, scribes, elders, and Sadducees as they sought to discredit Him with challenging questions. They questioned His authority, tried to snare Him on the issue of paying taxes to Caesar, and attempted to defeat Him with a theological dilemma concerning the resurrection. After Jesus refuted His opponents on each of these issues, He ended with a challenge of His own concerning their understanding of the Messiah that left them speechless.

READING OF LUKE 20

Prayer:

Lord, I marvel at the poise, brilliance, courage, wisdom, and insight of the Lord Jesus. May I never be so foolish as to question His authority or intentions in my life.

MEDITATION PASSAGE FOR TODAY:

verses 17–18, 25–26, 38

As He was teaching in the temple area, Jesus told His disciples not only about the coming destruction of the temple and the city of Jerusalem, but also about the signs that would precede His second advent. At the Passover meal in the upper room, the Lord spoke of the new covenant in His blood and once again predicted His betrayal, death, and coming kingdom. After His struggle in the Garden of Gethsemane, Jesus was betrayed, arrested, tried, and crucified.

Luke 24 concludes the narrative with the fulfillment of the glorious resurrection predicted in the Hebrew Bible and promised by Jesus. In the beautiful story of the road to Emmaus, the resurrected Jesus reveals Himself to two disciples after explaining to them the Messianic prophecies of Scripture.

READING OF LUKE 24

Prayer:

Lord, thank You for fulfilling the prophecies that the Messiah would suffer and rise again from the dead the third day, and that repentance for forgiveness of sins would be proclaimed in His name to all the nations.

MEDITATION PASSAGE FOR TODAY:

verses 5–7, 25–27, 32, 39, 44–47

DAY 231—JOHN 1

Matthew, Mark, and Luke are known collectively as the synoptic ("seeing together") gospels, because they share a common viewpoint and similar material. John, on the other hand, is a supplemental gospel, providing a wealth of stories and teachings of Jesus that are not found in the synoptics. The synoptic gospels, for example, focus on Christ's Galilean ministry, while John develops His Judean ministry.

The prologue (1:1–18) is one of the richest theological texts in Scripture: it reveals the eternality, divinity, and incarnation of the Word. This prologue is followed by an account of the witness of John the Baptist concerning Jesus and the story of Jesus' first disciples (1:19–51).

READING OF JOHN 1

Prayer:

Lord, I thank You for the mystery of the Word who became flesh and dwelt among us. I am grateful that while the Law was given through Moses, grace and truth were realized through Jesus Christ.

MEDITATION PASSAGE FOR TODAY:

verses 1–5, 10–18, 51

C hapters 2–12 present seven attesting signs that point to the Person and life-giving power of Jesus: (1) turning the water into wine (2:1–11); (2) healing the royal official's son (4:46–54); (3) healing the invalid (5:1–15); (4) feeding the multitude (6:1–14); (5) walking on water (6:16–21); (6) giving sight to the man born blind (9:1–41); and (7) raising Lazarus (11:1–45). In most cases, John follows these signs with a presentation of the reactions of belief and disbelief.

The story of Jesus' interview with Nicodemus points to the human need to be born of the Spirit in order to enjoy life with God. In John's testimony to Jesus, he saw himself as the friend of the bridegroom and affirmed that "He must increase, but I must decrease." This is the essence of the spiritual life.

READING OF JOHN 3

Prayer:

Lord, Your gift of eternal life to all who believe in Your Son is the highest expression of Your unbounded love for us. I ask that in my life, Jesus would increase and I would decrease.

MEDITATION PASSAGE FOR TODAY:

verses 3, 5–8, 14–21, 30, 35–36

O ur Lord always adapted Himself perfectly and graciously to the people He encountered. In John 3 He challenged Nicodemus to revisit the knowledge he should have had as a "teacher of Israel." But in John 4 He gradually reveals His true nature to an obscure woman at a well in Samaria. Even in speaking to her, Jesus overcomes three barriers: first, the racial barrier (Jews had no dealings with Samaritans); second, the gender barrier (Jewish rabbis would not address women as Jesus did); and third, the social barrier (this woman had a poor reputation among her own people). Jesus knew everything she had done, yet He gently and lovingly offered her the living water of eternal life.

READING OF JOHN 4

Prayer:

Lord, I give thanks that You know me through and through, and still You love me and desire intimacy with me. Give me the grace of holy desire so that I will respond eagerly to Your gracious and loving initiatives.

MEDITATION PASSAGE FOR TODAY:

verses 10, 13–14, 23–24

The seven "I am" statements in John's gospel combine to provide a profound portrait of the Lord Jesus: "I am the bread of life" (6:35); "I am the Light of the world" (8:12; 9:5); "I am the door of the sheep" (10:7, 9); "I am the good shepherd" (10:11, 14); "I am the resurrection and the life" (11:25); "I am the way, and the truth, and the life" (14:6); and "I am the true vine" (15:1–5).

Jesus listed five witnesses in 5:30–40 that bear witness to His authority and deity, and one of these witnesses is "the works which the Father has given me to accomplish." The feeding of the multitude, recorded in all four gospels, is a clear witness to the Person and power of Jesus, but His discourse on the bread of life caused many to leave Him when He related this bread to His flesh.

READING OF JOHN 6

Prayer:

Lord, I anchor my hope in Your promise that those who come to You will not hunger, and those who believe in You will never thirst; everyone who beholds Your Son and believes in Him will have eternal life, and He will raise them up on the last day.

MEDITATION PASSAGE FOR TODAY:

verses 27–29, 35–40, 51, 68–69

While all of the Gospels are thematic portraits, John is by far the most theological and selective. It also has the most unique material: 42% of Matthew, 7% of Mark, and 59% of Luke is unique to these gospels, but 92% of John is unique to John. In his narratives, John symbolically develops the theme of how those who were exposed to Jesus' words and works responded by either accepting or rejecting Him. Those who receive Him have eternal life (1:12; 3:16; 5:24; 10:27–29), while those who reject His offer remain under the condemnation of God (3:36; 5:25–29; 8:24). Jesus' controversy with His opponents in John 8 illustrates this rejection and ends with their attempt to stone Him when He associated himself with the divine I AM of the Old Testament (8:58; cf. 4:25–26; 8:24, 28; 13:19; 18:5–6, 8).

READING OF JOHN 8

Prayer:

Lord, because I have entrusted myself to Jesus, You have set me free from my slavery to sin and made me Your child forever.

MEDITATION PASSAGE FOR TODAY:

verses 12, 24, 28, 34–36, 58

The vocabulary and grammatical structure of the Gospel of John is simpler than the other gospels, but this gospel is more subtle and layered, and it is full of nuances and parallelism. While the synoptics all contain Jesus' parables, John uses allegories instead (e.g., the good shepherd in John 10 and the true vine in John 15).

In His allegory of the good shepherd, Jesus presents Himself as the gate by which the sheep may enter, the shepherd who is concerned for His flock and protects them, the one who knows His sheep and whose sheep know Him, and the lover of the flock who lays down His life for them. The Father is in Him, and He is in the Father, and the Father has sent Him into the world to purchase eternal life for the sheep His Father has given to Him.

READING OF JOHN 10

Prayer:

Lord, You are my shepherd, and I belong to Your flock. I look to You for all my needs, knowing that it is You who guide me, feed me, protect me, and give me the gift of eternal and abundant life.

MEDITATION PASSAGE FOR TODAY:

verses 7–11, 14–15, 18, 27–30

I n view of increasing hostility to His words and works, Jesus sees that His hour has finally come. At His last supper with the disciples, He prepares them for His imminent departure (13–16) and intercedes for them (17). The Upper Room Discourse, recorded only in John, is the most complete of Jesus' messages, and it contains the seed themes concerning the spiritual life that are later developed in the epistles.

Jesus, who loved and served His own until the end, gave His disciples a new commandment to love one another even as He loved them. Having washed the feet of His disciples (including Judas), Jesus predicted His betrayal. After Judas went out into the night, the Lord told His disciples of His imminent departure from this world.

READING OF JOHN 13

Prayer:

Lord, grant me Your power to love others even as You have loved me. May the love of the believers in my community be a demonstration that we are Your disciples.

MEDITATION PASSAGE FOR TODAY:

verses 1, 3, 13–15, 34–35

I n this portion of His Upper Room Discourse, Jesus prepares His disciples for His departure to the Father by assuring them of His continuing presence in their lives through the ongoing ministry of the Spirit of truth. He tells His own that He will prepare a place for them and then come again to receive them to Himself. Jesus exhorts them to love Him and keep His words so that He and the Father will love them and make Their abode with them. The deep mystery contained in the seven words, "You in Me, and I in you" speaks of the mutual indwelling that is the central truth and dynamic of the spiritual life. Jesus promises them a transcendent source of peace that can overcome their anxieties.

READING OF JOHN 14

Prayer:

Lord, I thank You for Your gift of the abiding Holy Spirit, for Your comforting words in a world of anxiety, for Your glorious promises, and for loving Your own and disclosing Yourself to us.

MEDITATION PASSAGE FOR TODAY:

verses 1–6, 11–15, 20–21, 23, 27

As Jesus leads His disciples to the Garden of Gethsemane, He relates the allegory of the vine and the branches to teach them about their need to abide in Him for their spiritual sustenance. It is only as they abide in Him that they will be empowered to bear abiding fruit, and it is this fruit that demonstrates their discipleship. Once again, Jesus commands them to love one another just as He loved them, and He emphasizes that it is not they who chose Him, but He who chose them. Because of their identification with Him, Jesus warns His disciples that the world will persecute them as it persecuted Him.

READING OF JOHN 15

Prayer:

Lord, You are the vinedresser, Jesus is the true vine, and I am a branch that desires to receive Christ's life by abiding in Him. May I abide in Your love, keep Your commandments, and love others as You have loved me.

MEDITATION PASSAGE FOR TODAY:

verses 1–17

K nowing that the time of His suffering and death is at hand, Jesus equips His disciples so that they will have perspective and power in their ministries after He returns to the Father. He tells them more about the Holy Spirit who will come to them, guide them into all the truth, and convict the world concerning sin, righteousness, and judgment. The Lord also prepares them for the suffering they will experience because of their testimony about Him. Though they will experience grief after His departure, their grief will turn into joy when they see Him again.

The disciples finally get a clear picture of what Jesus has been trying to teach them all along, and they declare that He came from God and knows all things.

READING OF JOHN 16

Prayer:

Lord, it is in You that I find true joy and peace. During my times of tribulation in this world I can take courage, because Jesus has overcome the world.

MEDITATION PASSAGE FOR TODAY:

verses 7–14, 23–24, 28, 33

I n this chapter, we are privileged to enter the most holy place of loving communion between the Father and the Son. In this high priestly prayer, offered just prior to the anguish of the garden, betrayal and arrest, trials, insults, beatings, and crucifixion, Jesus interceded on behalf of His disciples as well as those who believe in Him through their word. Now that He is about to leave the world, Jesus lifts up those who have been given to Him and asks His Father to "keep them in Your name, the name which You have given Me, that they may be one even as We are." Just as He is in the Father and the Father is in Him, so the Lord prays that those who have believed in Him would be perfected in unity and experience the mystery of "I in them, and You in Me."

READING OF JOHN 17

Prayer:

Lord, it is impossible for me to grasp the full implications of this holy prayer, since it expresses Your Son's desire that all who know Him will enter into the fullness of communion with the divine Trinity, the all in all.

MEDITATION PASSAGE FOR TODAY:

verses 3–4, 11, 16–18, 21–26

After a gripping account of Jesus' arrest, trials, and crucifixion (18–19), John provides a vivid narrative of several post-resurrection encounters between the Lord and His disciples (20–21). John's purpose statement is the clearest in Scripture: "But these have been written so that you may believe that Jesus is the Christ, the Son of God; and that believing you may have life in His name" (20:31). The beloved disciple selected the seven miraculous signs in 1–12 and the resurrection in 20–21 to bring the reader into an understanding of who Jesus is and to elicit a response of personal trust in Him.

Jesus' post-resurrection appearances to Mary Magdalene, the disciples without Thomas, and the disciples with Thomas were a source of unspeakable joy.

READING OF JOHN 20

Prayer:

Lord, I have believed that Jesus is the Christ, the Son of God, and I have found life in His name. As You have sent Him, so He also sends me.

MEDITATION PASSAGE FOR TODAY:

verses 17, 19–21, 26–31

A t His meeting with the disciples at the Sea of Galilee, Jesus restores Peter and commissions him to shepherd His sheep. John's gospel concludes by alluding to the abundance of things Jesus did that were never recorded.

As topical narratives, each of the four gospels approaches the life of Christ from a different angle. Matthew presents Him to a Jewish readership as Israel's Messiah-King, Mark presents Him to a Roman readership as the servant-redeemer, and Luke presents Him to a Greek readership as the perfect man. John, evidently written after the three synoptic gospels, presents Christ to a universal readership as the Son of God. The traditional picture of Christ in the four gospels relates to the imagery in Ezekiel 1:10 and Revelation 4:6–8 as follows: Matthew, a lion (strength, authority); Mark, an ox (service, power); Luke, a man (wisdom, character); John, an eagle (divinity).

READING OF JOHN 21

Prayer:

Lord, thank You for this marvelous account of Jesus' encounter with His disciples at the Sea of Galilee. I ask for the grace to follow Jesus wherever He leads me.

MEDITATION PASSAGE FOR TODAY:

verses 15–17, 25

The Great Commission in Matthew 28:19–20 to go and make disciples of all nations is supplemented by Christ's last words to His disciples before His ascension into heaven: "but you will receive power when the Holy Spirit has come upon you; and you shall be My witnesses both in Jerusalem, and in all Judea and Samaria, and even to the remotest part of the earth" (1:8). Luke wrote Acts to provide a historical link between the Gospels and the epistles. The account also chronicles the key events that brought about the birth and rapid spread of the church beginning in Jerusalem and moving beyond the borders of Israel to the other provinces of the Roman Empire.

The resurrected Lord instructs His disciples to wait in Jerusalem for the coming of the Holy Spirit who will empower them to be His witnesses. After Jesus ascends into heaven, the disciples choose Matthias to replace Judas as an apostle.

READING OF ACTS 1

Prayer:

Lord, it is Your Holy Spirit who empowers me to be Your witness to the people in my sphere of influence. May I live in such a way that they will be attracted to Jesus.

MEDITATION PASSAGE FOR TODAY:

verses 3–8

A cts continues the story of the birth of Christianity from the ascension of Christ to the time of Paul's first imprisonment in Rome. It serves as a crucial historical narrative that provides the backdrop to most of the epistles as it develops the exciting story of the birth and expansion of the early church which begins in Jerusalem, the city of the empty tomb, (1–7), spreads in the provinces of Judea and Samaria (8–12), and reaches throughout the Roman Empire (13–28).

When the Holy Spirit comes on the Day of Pentecost, Peter is empowered to deliver a sermon about the resurrected Christ that leads to the conversion of 3,000 listeners. All the sermons and defenses in Acts point to Jesus Christ as the resurrected Savior of the world. In his sermon in Acts 2, Peter builds upon Jesus' fulfillment of several Old Testament passages and points his listeners to the fact of the empty tomb to convict them that Jesus is both Lord and Christ (2:36).

READING OF ACTS 2

Prayer:

Lord, only the resurrection of Jesus and the indwelling power of the Holy Spirit can account for this radical transformation in the life of Peter. May I abide in the same hope and power.

MEDITATION PASSAGE FOR TODAY:

verses 22–24, 36–38, 42

After healing a man who was lame from birth, Peter delivers a convicting message to the people and another to the Sanhedrin (3–4). The church continues to grow, but the apostles are persecuted because of their message (5). Deacons are appointed to assist the apostles (6); then one of them, Stephen, speaks with such wisdom and authority that he is dragged before the Sanhedrin to be condemned. In his defense before the Jewish rulers, Stephen reviews the biblical narrative from the call of Abraham to the time of David and Solomon. Both Joseph and Moses were initially rejected by their people and later vindicated as God's deliverers, and Stephen charges that in the same way, the people have resisted the Holy Spirit by rejecting Jesus as their Messiah.

READING OF ACTS 7

Prayer:

Lord, by Your grace, may I not resist the work of the Holy Spirit in my life. I want to embrace Your good purposes for me and submit to Your loving authority.

MEDITATION PASSAGE FOR TODAY:

verses 55–56, 59–60

P hilip, another of the deacons selected in Acts 6, was led to proclaim Christ to the Samaritans who were viewed with disdain by the Jewish people. Philip's message was accompanied by attesting signs, and Simon the magician was attracted by these works of power. The apostles in Jerusalem sent Peter and John to Samaria to confer the gift of the Holy Spirit upon these new believers, but when Simon sought to buy the authority to impart this gift, Peter rebuked him for his wicked intentions.

Philip was directed by an angel to go to a desert road where he encountered an Ethiopian court official who was reading the Messianic prophecy in Isaiah 53. When Philip preached Jesus to him, he believed and was baptized.

READING OF ACTS 8

Prayer:

Lord, Your goodness and salvation extend to all who call upon Your name. May I be ready and faithful to share the good news about Your Son as Your Spirit gives me opportunity.

MEDITATION PASSAGE FOR TODAY:

verses 34–37

S aul, an approving witness of the martyrdom of Stephen (7:58; 8:1–3) was a young Pharisee who zealously ravaged the church in his opposition to followers of the Way. Not content with persecuting those who believed in Jesus in Judea, Saul obtained authority to go to Damascus to bring these followers of Jesus to trial in Jerusalem. His life was radically and permanently changed after his encounter with the resurrected Jesus on the road to Damascus, and he soon began to proclaim Jesus in the synagogues as the Son of God. Saul ministered for a time in Jerusalem until he was endangered and sent away to Tarsus.

The narrative switches back to Peter and relates the story of his healing of Aeneas in Lydda and his raising of Tabitha from the dead in Joppa.

READING OF ACTS 9

Prayer:

Lord, no one can oppose Your purposes and prevail. The Lord Jesus has all authority in heaven and earth, and His name will be proclaimed in the whole world as a testimony to all the nations until He comes to judge the world and reign in righteousness.

MEDITATION PASSAGE FOR TODAY:

verses 15–16, 31

The gospel of the resurrected Christ was first proclaimed to the Jews in Jerusalem and Judea, and then reached the Samaritan people. This crucial chapter records the first reception of the gospel among the Gentiles and marks the decisive point where Jews and Gentiles both become members of one body in Christ.

The Roman centurion Cornelius was a God-fearing man whose prayers and alms led to an angelic visitation in which he was instructed to dispatch men to Joppa to send for Peter. Meanwhile, Peter received three visions that prepared him to go willingly with the messengers to the house of Cornelius where he proclaimed that everyone who believes in Jesus receives forgiveness of sins. The Spirit of God came upon these Gentiles, and they were baptized in the name of Jesus Christ.

READING OF ACTS 10

Prayer:

Lord, the abundance of Your mercy and grace is available to everyone who seeks You. I acknowledge that Jesus is the Judge of the living and the dead, and that through His name everyone who believes in Him receives forgiveness of sins.

MEDITATION PASSAGE FOR TODAY:

verses 15, 34–35, 42–43

A cts is a highly selective historical account, and though it is sometimes called "The Acts of the Apostles," it is predominantly a series of important acts of Peter (1–12) and of Paul (13–28). This is a transitional book that explains how the composition of the church changed from being entirely Jewish (1–7) to a body that includes Samaritans and Gentiles (8–12); by the end of the 29 years covered in this book, the majority of believers in Christ were Gentiles.

In 13–28, Luke shifts his attention from Peter to Paul and gives an account of Paul's three missionary journeys, his trials, and his expedition to Rome. In the first missionary journey in A.D. 48–49 (13:1–14:28), Paul ministers in the province of Galatia.

READING OF ACTS 13

Prayer:

Lord, I thank You for Your glorious provision of forgiveness of sins and newness of life to all who transfer their trust from their own efforts to the perfect Person and work of the Lord Jesus.

MEDITATION PASSAGE FOR TODAY:

verses 38–39, 48, 52

After his first missionary journey, Paul and his co-laborer Barnabas returned to Syrian Antioch and reported to the church what God had done among the Gentiles. When some men from Judea argued that the Gentiles could not be saved unless they became proselytes to Judaism, Paul and Barnabas were sent to the apostles and elders in Jerusalem to resolve this crucial issue. Peter argued from his own experience that salvation is a gift of God for both Jews and Gentiles through the grace of the Lord Jesus and not through keeping of the Law of Moses. James concurred, so the apostles and elders sent Paul and Barnabas along with Judas and Silas to Antioch with a letter to confirm the council's conclusion.

READING OF ACTS 15

Prayer:

Lord, I give thanks that You make no distinction between people but make the same good news of forgiveness, cleansing, and grace available to all who turn to Jesus by faith.

MEDITATION PASSAGE FOR TODAY:

verses 7–11

Acts 15:36–18:22 records Paul's second missionary journey that took place in A.D. 50–52, in which Paul, accompanied this time by Silas, returned to Galatia, then proceeded beyond to Macedonia and Greece. Timothy soon joined them, and they strengthened the churches that had been established earlier. Heading north and then west, they reached Troas where Paul had a vision of a man of Macedonia who was calling for help. Responding to this call, they headed to Macedonia and made their way to Philippi. When Paul and Silas were beaten and thrown into an inner prison, their hymns of praise to God so affected the prisoners that none escaped when given an opportunity. This remarkable event led to the conversion of the Philippian jailer and his household.

READING OF ACTS 16

Prayer:

Lord, thank You for the simplicity and profundity of the good news that is encapsulated in the statement, "Believe in the Lord Jesus, and you will be saved." I entrust myself to Him and thank You for the gift of new life that He purchased for all who call upon Your name.

MEDITATION PASSAGE FOR TODAY:

verses 30–31

After leaving Philippi, Paul, Silas, and Timothy made their way to Thessalonica where a number of Jews and God-fearing Greeks came to faith in Jesus. The Jewish leaders stirred up the people against them, and Paul and his companions went on to Berea where the people "received the word with great eagerness" until agitators from Thessalonica turned the crowds against Paul. Silas and Timothy remained for a time in Berea while Paul journeyed to Athens where he reasoned in the synagogue and in the market place. When he was given an opportunity to address the Athenians on the Areopagus (Mars Hill), Paul told them about the one true God who "will judge the world in righteousness through a Man whom He has appointed, having furnished proof to all men by raising Him from the dead."

READING OF ACTS 17

Prayer:

Lord, You give to all people life and breath and all things; in You we live and move and exist. I give thanks that You have made it possible to know You through a relationship with Your Son Christ Jesus.

MEDITATION PASSAGE FOR TODAY:

verses 11, 24–31

P aul went on from Athens to Corinth where he continued his custom of bringing the gospel to the Jews first and then to the Gentiles. He allied himself with Aquila and his wife Priscilla, then when Silas and Timothy joined him, he devoted himself to proclaiming and teaching about Jesus the Messiah. Many of the Corinthians came to faith in Christ while Paul spent eighteen months teaching the word of God among them. Paul and his companions then sailed to Ephesus where he reasoned with the Jews in the synagogue. From there he sailed to Caesarea, went up to greet the church in Jerusalem, and returned to Antioch. After a time, Paul commenced his third missionary journey (A.D. 53–57; 18:23–21:16) by returning first to the region of Galatia and Phrygia to strengthen the disciples.

READING OF ACTS 18

Prayer:

Lord, I thank You for the prophecies in the Hebrew Bible that point to Jesus as the Messiah. May I come to know Him better by abiding in Him, entrusting myself to Him, and affirming His lordship over every component of my life.

MEDITATION PASSAGE FOR TODAY:

verses 5, 28

Paul continued west to Ephesus, the capital city of the Roman province of Asia, where he spent over two years teaching, reasoning daily, and performing miracles of healing. As the word of the Lord spread throughout Asia, Paul's opponents in Ephesus caused an uproar, so Paul decided to leave Ephesus to visit and exhort the churches in Macedonia and Greece. After a few months, he and his companions made their way back to Troas from which they sailed to Miletus where they met with the elders of the Ephesian church. Paul solemnly exhorted them, then set sail with his friends and journeyed on to Jerusalem. When some of Paul's Jewish opponents from Asia saw him in the temple, they stirred up the crowd against him. The mob dragged him out of the temple and began beating him until he was rescued by the soldiers under the Roman commander.

READING OF ACTS 21

Prayer:

Lord, Paul's passion for the gospel and his willingness to suffer deprivation, persecution, and death for the name of the Lord Jesus is both inspiring and challenging. May I be willing to endure hardship for the sake of His name.

MEDITATION PASSAGE FOR TODAY:

verses 13–14

When Paul was brought into the Roman barracks, he obtained permission from the commander to make his defense before the crowd. Addressing the people in Jewish Aramaic, Paul related how he persecuted the followers of the Way as a zealous Pharisee until his encounter with the resurrected Jesus on the road to Damascus. Ananias healed Paul's blindness and told him that he would be a witness to all of what he had seen and heard. But when Paul told the crowd about his divine commission to preach to the Gentiles, the people became furious and began shouting at him. The commander ordered that Paul be returned to the barracks and examined by scourging but changed his mind when Paul informed him of his Roman citizenship.

READING OF ACTS 22

Prayer:

Lord, I am reminded that the gospel of the Lord Jesus has never been neutral but cuts between those who seek You and those who turn away from You. May I be faithful to live for Jesus and to speak well of Him regardless of how people respond.

MEDITATION PASSAGE FOR TODAY:

verses 14–16

The Roman commander ordered the Sanhedrin to convene and set Paul before them to discover why he had been accused by the Jews. As a Pharisee, Paul quickly took advantage of the division between the Sadducees and the Pharisees over the issue of the resurrection from the dead which immediately caused a dissension between the two parties. Once again, the commander had to remove Paul to the safety of the Roman barracks. When Paul's nephew informed the commander of a conspiracy to kill Paul, he arranged to have Paul removed to Caesarea where his accusers could bring charges against him before Felix the governor. Felix read the commander's letter and arranged to give Paul a hearing after the arrival of his accusers.

READING OF ACTS 23

Prayer:

Lord, I take courage in the truth that no human opposition can defeat Your good purposes. May I trust You in difficult times, knowing that You always have my ultimate good at heart.

MEDITATION PASSAGE FOR TODAY:

verses 6, 11

Paul's accusers arrived in Caesarea and appeared before Felix, charging that he was a ringleader of a sect and was stirring up dissension among the Jews. When the governor gave Paul an opportunity to make his defense, the apostle argued that his opponents could give no proof of the charges they were making. He focused on the hope of the resurrection of the dead, a belief that is compatible with the Hebrew Scriptures. Felix decided to wait until Lysias the commander came down to Caesarea to decide Paul's case. For the next two years, however, Felix kept Paul in custody, allowing his friends to visit him, and often sent for him to converse with him. When Paul told the governor about faith in Christ Jesus, he came under conviction, but not to the point of repentance and faith.

READING OF ACTS 24

Prayer:

Lord, the biblical truths about righteousness, self-control, and the judgment to come can frighten hardened and powerful people, but only Your Holy Spirit can bring a person to the point of regeneration. May I rely on the power of Your Spirit in my walk and witness.

MEDITATION PASSAGE FOR TODAY:

verses 14–16, 25

A fter two years of imprisonment in Caesarea, Paul saw that the governor Felix was being succeeded by Festus. When the new governor went up to Jerusalem, Paul's opponents saw this as an opportunity to bring charges against him, hoping that he would be brought to Jerusalem so they could have him killed on the way. Festus invited them to come to Caesarea to prosecute Paul. When Paul was brought out before them, the new governor asked Paul if he was willing to stand trial in Jerusalem. Knowing what this would mean, Paul exercised his right as a Roman citizen to appeal to Caesar. When King Agrippa and Bernice arrived at Caesarea to visit Festus, the governor arranged for them to hear Paul, hoping to clarify the charges he would write before sending the prisoner to the Emperor.

READING OF ACTS 25

Prayer:

Lord, the plots and devices of men will never prevail against Your purposes and promises. May I imitate Paul's faith by taking the long-term perspective, and thus live by faith and hope.

MEDITATION PASSAGE FOR TODAY:

verses 8, 11

The apostle took full advantage of his opportunity to present his defense before King Agrippa and argued that the hope of the resurrection from the dead is fully in accord with the prophetic writings revered by the Jews. Paul recounted his efforts as a Pharisee to persecute the followers of Jesus of Nazareth and his encounter with Jesus Himself on the way to Damascus. He then related his commission to proclaim to both Jews and Gentiles the message of forgiveness of sins through faith in Jesus. When Paul argued that Moses and the prophets predicted these things about the Messiah, Festus accused Paul of madness. The apostle appealed to Agrippa's knowledge of the Jewish prophets, but the king shrugged it off and told Festus afterward that Paul could have been released if he had not appealed to Caesar.

READING OF ACTS 26

Prayer:

Lord, I give thanks for the life-giving message that turns people from darkness to light and from the dominion of Satan to God, that they may receive forgiveness of sins and an inheritance among those who have been sanctified by faith in Jesus.

MEDITATION PASSAGE FOR TODAY:

verses 18–20, 22–23

P aul and other prisoners were delivered to a Roman centurion named Julius who made arrangements to bring them by
ship to Rome. After they sailed to Lycia, Julius put his soldiers
and prisoners on a ship that was bound for Italy. As this portion of the trip became increasingly treacherous, they arrived
at Crete where Paul warned them not to continue on. Hoping
to make it to a suitable harbor for wintering, however, Julius
decided with the majority to continue on. After their ship was
caught in a violent storm and all hope of being saved was lost,
Paul related an angelic message he received that he would stand
before Caesar and that none of them would perish in the sea.
Paul also predicted that they would run aground on an island.
When this occurred, all of them were brought safely to land.

READING OF ACTS 27

Prayer:

*Lord, Your word never fails, and You accomplish all the things
You promise to Your saints. May I cling to You during the
storms of life and hope in Your life-giving promises.*

MEDITATION PASSAGE FOR TODAY:

verses 24–25

T he 276 people from the shipwreck found themselves on the island of Malta where the natives kindled a fire to warm them against the cold and the rain. When a viper bit Paul on the hand, and they observed that he suffered no harm, the natives began to say that he was a god. After Publius generously entertained his new guests and Paul healed the father of Publius, the rest of the people on the island came to Paul for healing. At the end of three months, Paul and the others embarked on a ship that had wintered at the island then finally arrived at the port of Puteoli in Italy, south of Rome. Paul was brought to Rome where he was placed under house arrest to await his trial before Caesar. He gathered the leading members of the Jewish community to explain his circumstances and to explain from the Scriptures that Jesus is the promised Messiah.

READING OF ACTS 28

Prayer:

Lord, I ask for the wisdom, boldness, and open doors to testify about the kingdom of God and the Lord Jesus Christ with sensitivity and clarity.

MEDITATION PASSAGE FOR TODAY:

verses 23, 31

While the Gospels portray the words and works of Jesus Christ, the book of Romans develops the profound implications of His life, death, and resurrection for those who trust in Him. Romans is the most systematic and comprehensive theological treatise in the Bible, presenting the powerful themes of salvation, righteousness, faith, justification, redemption, atonement, reconciliation, and imputation with greater clarity than anywhere else in Scripture. Romans 6–8 is the supreme passage for the meaning of the spiritual life, and Romans 12–14 is crucial to our understanding of the outworking of the spiritual life.

The theme of Romans, spelled out in 1:16–17, is that the gospel is the power of God for salvation and righteousness for those whose faith is in Jesus Christ.

READING OF ROMANS 1

Prayer:

Lord, You have revealed Yourself to all people through Your vast and marvelous created order, yet so many people have turned away from the glory of the incorruptible God to worship and serve the creature. May I always honor You as God and give thanks.

MEDITATION PASSAGE FOR TODAY:

verses 3–4, 16–20

During his stay in Corinth near the end of his third missionary journey in A.D. 57, Paul wrote this magnificent epistle to the well-known and influential church in Rome which he had not yet visited. Paul launches his epistle with a prologue that states his intention of coming to Rome, as well as his theme of righteousness (conformity to God's character) before God through faith in Christ (1:1–17). He then develops an unanswerable case for the universal condemnation of both Gentiles and Jews in view of their sinful condition of falling short of the righteousness of God (1:18–3:20).

Having demonstrated the condemnation of the Gentiles in chapter 1, Paul does the same regarding both the moral Jew and the religious Jew in chapter 2. The human conscience reveals that people cannot even live up to their own moral standards.

READING OF ROMANS 2

Prayer:

Lord, I know that whenever I judge another, I condemn myself, since I cannot even keep my own moral standards, let alone those revealed in Your Word. May I keep my eyes on Your Son rather than on the shortcomings of others.

MEDITATION PASSAGE FOR TODAY:

verses 1, 14–16

Having indicted both the Gentiles and the Jews, the apostle completes his portrait of universal condemnation before a holy God with a series of quotations from the Psalms. The Law demonstrates the knowledge of sin, but it does not provide a solution.

God's solution to this universal human dilemma is found in the redemption and atoning work of Jesus Christ. Faith in Him rather than works is the key to appropriating His offer by which we are justified (declared righteous) by God Himself (3:21–31). While "all have sinned and fall short of the glory of God," we are "justified as a gift by His grace through the redemption which is in Christ Jesus."

READING OF ROMANS 3

Prayer:

Lord, You have paid the price of redemption through the blood of Your Son, and it is through faith in Him that I have received the grace of being justified in Your sight.

MEDITATION PASSAGE FOR TODAY:

verses 20, 23–28

DAY 266—ROMANS 4

P aul uses the experience of David and the life of Abraham to illustrate the principle of justification by faith apart from works. It was through the righteousness of faith that Abraham was justified. This took place prior to Abraham's circumcision in order that he would be the father of all who believe, whether they are Jews or Gentiles. Abraham believed God's promise concerning his descendants ("Then he believed in the Lord; and He reckoned it to him as righteousness"; Genesis 15:6), though this faith in the promise of God was contrary to human appearances. Thus, Abraham became the exemplar for all "who believe in Him who raised Jesus our Lord from the dead."

READING OF ROMANS 4

Prayer:

Lord, I thank You for Abraham's faith in You and in Your promise to him, even though it appeared impossible to fulfill. I am grateful that when I put my trust in Jesus, this faith was credited to me as righteousness.

MEDITATION PASSAGE FOR TODAY:

verses 3–5, 17, 24–25

J ustification by faith leads to peace and reconciliation with God (5:1–11). Reconciliation speaks of the change in our state of alienation from God because of the redemptive work of His Son on our behalf. It is made possible through God's love which is causeless (5:6), measureless (5:7–8), and ceaseless (5:9–11). In 5:12–21, Paul contrasts the two Adams and the opposite results of their two acts. The disobedience of the first Adam made him the head of all who are under sin, but the obedience of the second Adam made Him the head of the race of redeemed humanity. The sin of the first Adam was imputed to us (placed on our account), leading to alienation. But the righteousness of Christ is imputed to all who trust in Him, leading to reconciliation.

READING OF ROMANS 5

Prayer:

Lord, Your love has been poured out within our hearts through the Holy Spirit who was given to us. You demonstrated Your own love toward us, in that while we were yet sinners, Christ died for us.

MEDITATION PASSAGE FOR TODAY:

verses 1–8, 20–21

Romans presents Christ as the Savior and Redeemer whose atoning work on the cross has made it possible for God to "be just and the justifier of the one who has faith in Jesus" (3:26). He is the second Adam whose obedience has overcome the sin and separation wrought by the disobedience of the first Adam (5:12–21). It is through our identification with Him in His death, burial, and resurrection that we enjoy freedom from the dominion of sin and newness of life (6:1–23). The reality of union with Christ is the basis for the spiritual walk. Believers must know their position in Christ, regard it as true, and present themselves to God as dead to sin but alive to God in Christ Jesus. Paul views devotion as a response to spiritual truth, not as a condition of it.

READING OF ROMANS 6

Prayer:

Lord, I acknowledge by faith that I have been united with Your Son in His death, burial, and resurrection, and that in Christ I am no longer a slave to sin. I present myself to You as one alive from the dead, and my members as instruments of righteousness to You.

MEDITATION PASSAGE FOR TODAY:

verses 3–14, 23

DAY 269—ROMANS 7

The apostle argues that the only way we can be released from the jurisdiction of the law is to die, and that our death in Christ to that by which we were bound enables us to "serve in newness of the Spirit and not in oldness of the letter." He goes on to say that the Mosaic Law was given in order to reveal the problem of indwelling sin and our condition of separation from the holiness of God.

In 7:14–25 Paul speaks of the conflict that believers in Christ experience between the "inner man" (the new nature we have received in Christ) and the "flesh" or "the law of sin which is in my members." This inward/outward conflict between the new and the old dispositions will not be eliminated until we are in our resurrected bodies.

READING OF ROMANS 7

Prayer:

Lord, I joyfully concur with the law of God in my inner being in Christ, but I see a different law in the members of my body. May I walk in union with Christ and in the power of Your Spirit.

MEDITATION PASSAGE FOR TODAY:

verses 4, 6, 22–25

F ollowers of Christ have two present resources to give them victory in the painful inward/outward conflict described in 7:14–25. The first is our identification with Christ in His death, burial, and resurrection life (Romans 6), and the second is the indwelling presence of the Holy Spirit (Romans 8). People who have turned from their sins (repentance) and trusted in Christ (faith) are indwelled by the Spirit of Him who raised Christ Jesus from the dead. When we set our minds on the Spirit, we walk in His life and peace.

Having dealt with the issues of our condemnation (1:18–3:20), our justification (3:21–5:21), and our sanctification (6:1–8:17), Paul looks ahead to our glorification (8:18–39). All believers can anticipate a time when they will be perfectly conformed to Jesus Christ not only in their position (present) but also in their practice (the future resurrection).

READING OF ROMANS 8

Prayer:

Lord, I praise You that neither death, nor life, nor angels, nor principalities, nor things present, nor things to come, nor powers, nor height, nor depth, nor any other created thing, will be able to separate me from Your love in Christ Jesus my Lord.

MEDITATION PASSAGE FOR TODAY:

verses 1–6, 9–18, 26–30, 38–39

In chapters 1–8, Paul unfolds God's sovereign plan of salvation, and in chapters 9–11, he deals with the question of God's relationship to Israel now that the Gentiles have the same access as the Jews to Israel's Messiah. The third section, chapters 12–16, focuses on the application of life in Christ to various practical aspects of daily experience.

The apostle recognizes that behavior must be built upon belief, which is why the practical exhortations of this epistle appear after his teaching on the believer's position in Christ. Personal consecration (12:1–2) should lead to corporate transformation (12:3–21); the dynamic of our faith in Christ must be expressed in other-centered relationships in the body of Christ.

READING OF ROMANS 12

Prayer:

Lord, because of all You have done for me, I present my body to You as a living sacrifice. I want to be transformed by the renewing of my mind, affirming that Your will for me is good and acceptable and perfect.

MEDITATION PASSAGE FOR TODAY:

verses 1–5, 9–18

The salvation described in the first eleven chapters should transform a believer's life in relation to God (12:1–2), ministry to the body of Christ (12:3–8), social relationships (12:9–21), submission to governing authorities (13:1–7), and the needs of others (13:8–15:13).

Paul argues that in spite of their flaws, governing authorities are established by God who raises them up and deposes them. It is only when a government overreaches its divinely-given sphere of authority that followers of Jesus can stand in opposition. Romans 13 concludes with an affirmation that love is the fulfillment of the law, and with an exhortation to live in view of the future by putting on the armor of light.

READING OF ROMANS 13

Prayer:

Lord, may I lay aside the deeds of darkness and put on the armor of light. I want to put on the Lord Jesus Christ and make no provision for the flesh in regard to its lusts.

MEDITATION PASSAGE FOR TODAY:

verses 8, 10, 12–14

One of the purposes of this epistle was to encourage the Jews and Gentiles in the church in Rome to develop a spirit of unity in one body. To this end, Paul outlines the principles and practice of Christian liberty as this relates to different levels of spiritual maturity. Concerning matters of conscience rather than command, those who cannot indulge should not judge those who can, and those who can indulge should not look down on those who cannot. At the same time, those who have faith in these areas should voluntarily restrict themselves when in the presence of those who do not, so they will not cause the latter to stumble. In all things we are to "pursue the things which make for peace and the building up of one another."

READING OF ROMANS 14

Prayer:

Lord, thank You for this reminder that the kingdom of God is not eating and drinking, but righteousness and peace and joy in the Holy Spirit.

MEDITATION PASSAGE FOR TODAY:

verses 7–10, 17, 19, 22

When Paul wrote this epistle, he wanted to prepare the Christians in Rome for his planned visit to them (which was delayed by his two-year imprisonment in Caesarea) and to ground them in the knowledge of the faith. Paul also wanted to solicit the prayer support of these believers in the Imperial City at a transitional point in his ministry in which he had completed his apostolic task of laying the foundation for the gospel in the eastern provinces and was now hoping to do the same in the western provinces.

Paul informed his Roman readers, some of whom he had already met in his travels (16:1–15), of his intention to visit them after he completed his mission of delivering a collection from the churches of Macedonia and Achaia to the poor among the saints in Jerusalem (15:20–29).

READING OF ROMANS 15

Prayer:

Lord, I ask that You, the God of hope, will fill me with all joy and peace in believing, so that I will abound in hope by the power of the Holy Spirit.

MEDITATION PASSAGE FOR TODAY:

verses 1–7, 13

F irst Corinthians is a very practical treatise on the application of Christian principles to a wide variety of personal and corporate issues, including the need for unity rather than divisiveness in the body of believers, church discipline for sexual immorality, the problem of litigation between believers, counsel concerning marriage, liberty regarding doubtful things, public worship and the use of spiritual gifts, and the nature of the resurrection.

Paul's first concern in this letter is the problem of false pride and divisiveness caused by focusing on people rather than the Lord (1:1–17). Human wisdom is totally inadequate; only the power and wisdom of God can bring salvation (1:18–31).

READING OF 1 CORINTHIANS 1

Prayer:

Lord, it is by Your doing that we are in Christ Jesus, who became to us wisdom from God, and righteousness and sanctification, and redemption. May I boast only in You.

MEDITATION PASSAGE FOR TODAY:

verses 10, 18, 21–31

C orinth was a thriving center of commerce with two seaports strategically located on a narrow isthmus between the Aegean and the Adriatic Seas. This city was also a center of idolatry and immorality where pleasure seekers would come to be entertained. During his second missionary journey, Paul established a church in this corrupt city and taught the Scriptures there for 18 months in A.D. 51–52. In A.D. 56 Paul wrote this epistle to the church at Corinth (5:9 indicates that he had written at least one previous letter to them) on his third missionary journey near the end of his years of ministry in the city of Ephesus (16:5–8).

In chapter 2 Paul argues that the gospel transcends human wisdom and must be spiritually discerned, since it cannot be grasped by the natural mind.

READING OF 1 CORINTHIANS 2

Prayer:

Lord, I thank You for Your indwelling Spirit who leads me into a knowledge of the truth about Jesus, the Lord of glory. I rest my faith not on the wisdom of men, but on the power of God.

MEDITATION PASSAGE FOR TODAY:

verses 5, 9, 14–16

The church at Corinth was plagued by an immature and divisive spirit as various members oriented themselves around human personalities rather than the Person and work of Christ. Paul therefore exhorts them to focus on the Lord rather than His servants. Using an agricultural metaphor, Paul says that it is God who causes the growth. Switching to an architectural metaphor, the apostle argues that Jesus Christ is the foundation upon which we must build. As we build on this foundation, we will be rewarded for that which endures on the day when God tests the quality of our work. Since the Holy Spirit dwells in us, we should walk in the wisdom of looking to Jesus rather than being impressed by people.

READING OF 1 CORINTHIANS 3

Prayer:

Lord, may I find my identity, dignity, and worth in Christ Jesus rather than in the superficial things that may impress people, but are passing away.

MEDITATION PASSAGE FOR TODAY:

verses 6–7, 11–17, 21–23

Having dealt with the problem of factions in the church (1:1–4:21), Paul turns to the problem of incest between a member of the church and his stepmother and exhorts the church to exercise corporate discipline by removing the offender from their fellowship until he repents (5:1–13). The third problem is that of litigation between believers. Paul instructs them to settle their differences among themselves without resorting to the civil courts (6:1–8). The fourth problem Paul addresses in this epistle is that of sexual immorality (6:9–20). He argues that since the believer's body is a temple of the Holy Spirit, we must flee immorality and glorify God in our bodies.

READING OF 1 CORINTHIANS 6

Prayer:

Lord, I give thanks that I was washed, sanctified, and justified in the name of the Lord Jesus Christ and in the Spirit of my God. Since I have been bought with a price, may I glorify You in my body.

MEDITATION PASSAGE FOR TODAY:

verses 2, 11–12, 19–20

I n chapters 7–16, Paul discusses specific questions that have been raised and offers spiritual perspectives on four areas. First, he takes up the issues of marriage, celibacy, divorce, and remarriage in chapter 7. The apostle affirms the place of marriage in the economy of God but at the same time teaches that those who have the gift of celibacy would do better not to marry in order that they may be focused on the things of the Lord. Those who are married do not have authority over their own bodies but should seek to please their spouse. Those who are called to remain unmarried have the advantage of "undistracted devotion to the Lord" which Paul regards as an advantage in view of Christ's imminent return.

READING OF 1 CORINTHIANS 7

Prayer:

Lord, You distribute Your gifts and callings in ways that are uniquely appropriate to each of Your people. May I seek to please You and to be faithful to Your calling in my life.

MEDITATION PASSAGE FOR TODAY:

verses 4, 7, 17, 29–31

The second question Paul discusses is the problem of eating food offered to idols and the importance of doing all things to the glory of God as well as the edification of others (8:1–11:1). The apostle states that those who know that there is but one God and that idols are meaningless are at liberty to partake of food that had been offered in the pagan temples. However, he warns these Christians not to allow their liberty to become a stumbling block for those who do not have this knowledge. Knowledge by itself can make one arrogant if it is not tempered by the love of Christ that seeks to nurture other people. Thus, it is better not to exercise one's freedom in cases where this would cause another's conscience to be wounded.

READING OF 1 CORINTHIANS 8

Prayer:

Lord, I acknowledge that there is but one God, the Father, from whom are all things, and I exist for Him. I acknowledge there is but one Lord, Jesus Christ, by whom are all things, and I exist through Him.

MEDITATION PASSAGE FOR TODAY:

verses 1–3, 6

P aul uses his own life to illustrate the twin principles of liberty in Christ and the law of love. As an apostle, he has a right to receive his living from the ministry of the word, but to prevent the Corinthians from stumbling over the issue of his "charging" for the gospel, Paul chose to work for his living while he was in their midst. As he argued in Romans 14, believers must sometimes limit their liberty for the sake of those whose faith is weaker.

Paul did everything for the sake of the gospel, including adapting himself to varying circumstances in order to gain common ground without compromise. Although he understood his liberty, he disciplined himself so that he would not be disqualified from being rewarded at the end of his race.

READING OF 1 CORINTHIANS 9

Prayer:

Lord, as I grow in understanding of my true freedom in Christ, may I also consider the needs of others and limit my liberty, when necessary, to display the love of Jesus to them.

MEDITATION PASSAGE FOR TODAY:

verses 19–23

T he third question Paul addresses relates to public worship, including improper observance of the Lord's Supper and the selfish use of spiritual gifts (11:2–14:40). The apostle teaches that the body of Christ is a unity within diversity, and that the multiplicity of spiritual gifts must be exercised in love for the edification of the whole body.

This great chapter on love is sandwiched right in the middle of Paul's teaching concerning the use and abuse of spiritual gifts. Even the most dramatic gifts and sacrificial deeds are useless and dead if they are not animated by God's love. All these gifts will be done away when we see the Lord face to face, but love will abide.

READING OF 1 CORINTHIANS 13

Prayer:

Lord, the love that comes from You is patient, kind, and not jealous; it does not brag and is not arrogant, does not act unbecomingly; it does not seek its own, is not provoked, does not take into account a wrong suffered, does not rejoice in unrighteousness, but rejoices with the truth; bears all things, believes all things, hopes all things, endures all things.

MEDITATION PASSAGE FOR TODAY:

verses 4–7, 13

T he fourth question Paul discusses concerns misunder-
standings about the resurrection. Paul's historical and
theological defense of the resurrection includes teaching on the
nature of the resurrection body. The Corinthians evidently have
been struggling over this issue because the idea of a resurrected
body is disdainful in Greek thought. Paul recounts the post-
resurrection appearances of Jesus and argues that if there is no
resurrection of the dead, Christ has not been raised and we are
still in our sins. But because He has been raised, He has abol-
ished death, the last enemy, and has assured us that our per-
ishable and natural bodies will be raised as imperishable and
spiritual bodies. Because this mortal will put on immortality,
we live in the hope that our toil is not in vain in the Lord.

READING OF 1 CORINTHIANS 15

Prayer:

*Lord, I rejoice in the hope of the resurrected, glorious, imperish-
able, spiritual, heavenly immortality that You promise to all
who have entrusted themselves to Your resurrected Son.*

MEDITATION PASSAGE FOR TODAY:

verses 3–4, 20–22, 42–44, 51–54, 58

S econd Corinthians is an intensely personal epistle that reveals the heart of the apostle Paul, his motives for ministry, and the way he conducted himself in the service of others. His defense of the integrity of his ministry with the Corinthians in the face of attacks and wrongful allegations by false teachers gives us a model for the way we should pursue integrity, so that even if we are impugned, we will have a clear conscience before God and a faithful record before people.

Although the majority of believers in Corinth repented of their opposition to Paul's apostolic authority, there was still an unrepentant minority, evidently led by a group of Judaizers (10–13), who continued to challenge him. Paul wrote this epistle to defend his conduct, character, and apostolic calling. This is the primary theme that ties this letter together, even in the portion that was addressed to the repentant majority (1–9).

READING OF 2 CORINTHIANS 1

Prayer:

Lord, You are the Father of mercies and God of all comfort. I thank You for comforting me in my affliction so that I will be able to comfort others also.

MEDITATION PASSAGE FOR TODAY:

verses 3–4, 21–22

P aul begins this epistle with thanksgiving for God's comfort in his hardships (1:1–11) and then explains that his delay in visiting the Corinthians was not due to wavering, but to give them sufficient time to repent (1:12–2:4). He asks them to restore the repentant offender (2:5–13) and goes on to defend the conduct, content, and motivation of his ministry among them (2:14–6:10). After an exhortation to be separate from defilement (6:11–7:1), Paul describes the encouragement he received from Titus' report (7:2–16).

In spite of the many adversities he has encountered, Paul does not lose heart because he has developed an eternal perspective on temporal affliction. As he wrote in Romans 8:18, "I consider that the sufferings of this present time are not worthy to be compared with the glory that is to be revealed to us."

READING OF 2 CORINTHIANS 4

Prayer:

Lord, thank You that momentary, light affliction is producing for me an eternal weight of glory far beyond all comparison. May I set my heart on the things which are not seen.

MEDITATION PASSAGE FOR TODAY:

verses 6–7, 16–18

Day 286—2 Corinthians 5

T his important chapter reveals important truths concerning
the resurrection and judgment of believers (5:1–10), and
the meaning and ministry of reconciliation (5:11–21). Although
"there is now no condemnation for those who are in Christ
Jesus" (Romans 8:1), believers will still appear before the judgment seat of Christ to be rewarded according to their works. It
is wise to remember the brevity of our temporal sojourn so that
we will invest our earthly time wisely before we are at home
with the Lord. We have been called to a ministry of reconciliation in our spheres of influence as ambassadors for Christ. When
we leave this planet, we will never again have the opportunity
of sharing the gospel or serving the needy.

READING OF 2 CORINTHIANS 5

Prayer:
*Lord, You made Jesus who knew no sin to be sin on our behalf,
so that we might become the righteousness of God in Him.*

MEDITATION PASSAGE FOR TODAY:
verses 6–10, 14–17, 21

The apostle appeals to the Corinthians to follow the Macedonians' example of generosity by keeping their promise of contributing to the collection he was planning to bring to the believers in Judea (8–9). These two chapters develop the central New Testament teaching on financial stewardship and illustrate a number of timeless principles.

Just as the believers in Macedonia gave with a sense of joyful participation in spite of their meager resources, so Paul encourages the Corinthians to be participants in the gracious work of God in contributing to the needs of others. When we give ourselves first to the Lord (verse 5), then we are empowered to give ourselves to others by the will of God.

READING OF 2 CORINTHIANS 8

Prayer:

Lord, I glory in the grace of our Lord Jesus Christ, that though He was rich, yet for our sake He became poor, so that we through His poverty might become rich.

MEDITATION PASSAGE FOR TODAY:

verses 3, 5, 9, 14, 21

H aving mentioned the example of the Macedonians' liberal giving for the needy brethren in Jerusalem (8:1–6), Paul appealed to the Corinthians to keep their promise by doing the same (8:7–9:15). In this connection, Paul commends the messengers he has sent to Corinth to make arrangements for the large gift they have promised. The apostle assures them that their generosity will be more than amply rewarded by God.

Paul urges his readers not only to be bountiful in their giving, but to give out of a cheerful rather than grudging heart. In the same way, God is able to make all grace abound to them and to make them sufficient in everything.

READING OF 2 CORINTHIANS 9

Prayer:

Lord, You are able to make all grace abound to me so that, always having all sufficiency in everything, I may have an abundance for every good deed. Thanks be to You for Your indescribable gift!

MEDITATION PASSAGE FOR TODAY:

verses 6–8, 15

T urning his attention to the unrepentant minority who continued to challenge his authority, Paul defends his apostolic calling and credentials (10–13). His meekness in their presence does not minimize his authority (10), and though he is loath to boast about them, his knowledge, honesty, achievements, persecutions, visions, and miraculous signs all vindicate his apostolic claims (11–12:13). He concludes by telling of his plans for a third visit and warns them to repent before he comes (12:14–13:14).

Paul's vision of being caught up into Paradise led to his thorn in the flesh as God's means of keeping him weak so that he could minister out of Christ's power rather than his own.

READING OF 2 CORINTHIANS 12

Prayer:

Lord, Your grace is sufficient for me, for power is perfected in weakness. May I walk and serve through dependence on Your power rather than my own resources.

MEDITATION PASSAGE FOR TODAY:

verses 9–10, 19

The gospel of grace as opposed to the trap of works-based religiosity finds its clearest exposition in the epistle to the Galatians. There is a natural human tendency to suppose that we can or must earn God's approval, acceptance, love, or forgiveness through our own effort and achievement. It is not uncommon, even for those who understand that salvation is a gift of God's grace through faith in Christ Jesus, to slip into the error of thinking that spiritual growth is primarily a matter of human effort and merit. Galatians corrects this error by stressing that the same principle that brings about our justification (grace through faith) also brings about our sanctification. When we walk by the Spirit, we are empowered to bear the spiritual fruit of love, joy, peace, patience, kindness, goodness, faithfulness, gentleness, and self-control.

READING OF GALATIANS 5

Prayer:

Lord, may I walk in the power of Your Holy Spirit by abiding in Christ Jesus. I desire to display the fruit of the Spirit rather than the deeds of the flesh.

MEDITATION PASSAGE FOR TODAY:

verses 5, 13–14, 16, 22–25

Paul begins this epistle with a biographical argument (1–2) that affirms the divine origin of his apostleship and his message of the gospel of grace in contrast to the distortion of the gospel by false teachers. He recounts how God gave him the message of justification by faith in Christ and how this was confirmed by the apostles. Paul then develops a theological argument (3–4) in defense of justification by faith, contending that the law was given not to save people, but to bring them to faith. The apostle concludes with a moral argument (5–6) that anticipates the objection that the liberty of grace could degenerate into license and lawlessness. Paul insists that faith expressing itself through love and empowered by the Holy Spirit will overcome the propensities of the flesh and fulfill the requirements of the law.

READING OF GALATIANS 6

Prayer:

Lord, may I never boast except in the cross of our Lord Jesus Christ, through which the world has been crucified to me, and I to the world.

MEDITATION PASSAGE FOR TODAY:

verses 2, 7–10, 14

M ost believers have only a vague notion of their true identity and spiritual wealth, so as a consequence, they live like spiritual paupers without appropriating the marvelous resources that God has placed at their disposal. They are frustrated when they hear messages that tell them how they ought to order their lives because they do not know how to accomplish this; then even when they try, they do not succeed. The first half of Ephesians (1–3) offers a solution to this dilemma by exposing us to the treasury of spiritual blessings that are already ours in Christ if we will lay hold of them by faith in His promises. By looking to Him for our identity and empowerment, we discover that it is possible through His grace to fulfill the commands that are developed in the second half of Ephesians (4–6).

READING OF EPHESIANS 1

Prayer:

Lord, I pray that You will give me a spirit of wisdom and of revelation in the true knowledge of our Lord Jesus Christ.

MEDITATION PASSAGE FOR TODAY:

verses 3–14, 17–19

DAY 293—EPHESIANS 2

Our position in Christ (1–3) lays the foundation for our practice in Christ (4–6). After a prologue, Paul praises the triune God for the work of the Father in choosing us (1:3–6), the Son in redeeming us (1:7–12), and the Spirit for sealing us (1:13–14). This marvelous hymn to God's grace is followed by a prayer for spiritual illumination in the knowledge of our calling, inheritance, and power (1:15–23). Paul contrasts his readers' former spiritual condition without Christ with the life and hope that salvation by grace through faith has given them (2:1–10). This redemption includes Jews, yet it also extends to Gentiles who previously were "strangers to the covenants of promise." In Christ, the two for the first time have become "fellow citizens with the saints" and members of one body (2:11–22).

READING OF EPHESIANS 2

Prayer:

Lord, I thank You that it is by grace that we have been saved through faith; and that not of ourselves, it is the gift of God, not as a result of works, so that no one may boast.

MEDITATION PASSAGE FOR TODAY:

verses 4–10

Day 294—Ephesians 3

E phesians as a whole, and especially the first three chapters, is full of rich imagery and thought, developing insights about the believer's position in Christ that are both profound and powerful. The two prayers in this book (1:15–23; 3:14–21) are among the most significant in the Bible, and they can be used with great profit. The unification of Jew and Gentile in one body was formerly a mystery that has now become manifest (3:1–13). In his second prayer, Paul asks that his readers be strengthened with God's power and with the knowledge of the love of Christ (3:14–21).

Paul wrote this epistle to encourage his readers to grow into spiritual maturity by laying hold of the resources they have in Christ and by building each other up through the use of spiritual gifts and through serving one another out of Christ's love.

READING OF EPHESIANS 3

Prayer:

Lord, I ask that You would strengthen me with power through Your indwelling Spirit so that Christ may dwell in my heart through faith, and that I would be rooted and grounded in His love.

MEDITATION PASSAGE FOR TODAY:

verses 16–21

P aul's theme in Ephesians is captured in the pivotal verse that links the two major sections together: "Therefore I, the prisoner of the Lord, implore you to walk in a manner worthy of the calling with which you have been called" (4:1). This remarkable chapter about the unity and diversity of the body of Christ marks the application of the glorious truths about our true position in Christ in Ephesians 1–3. Paul's passion was that people would not only understand who they are in their vertical relationship with Christ, but also express this new identity in their horizontal relationships with one another. The gifts of the Holy Spirit were given to empower us to serve other members of the body in such a way that we build each other up and grow together in ever-greater maturity and Christlike character. By "speaking the truth in love" we encourage and equip others to "grow up in all aspects into Him."

READING OF EPHESIANS 4

Prayer:

Lord, I want to be renewed in the spirit of my mind and put on the righteousness and true holiness of the new creation I have become in Christ. Please empower me to love and serve others in such a way that they will be built up and encouraged in Him.

MEDITATION PASSAGE FOR TODAY:

verses 4–7, 15, 22–24, 32

I n the second half of Ephesians, Paul turns from the privileges of the believer to the responsibilities of the believer. He exhorts his readers to grow in unity and in maturity through the loving exercise of their spiritual gifts (4:1–16). He calls them to walk in the power of the new self and to practice righteousness, truth, self-control, and forgiveness (4:17–32). As God's beloved children, they are to live in the light and avoid the deeds of darkness (5:1–21). Their relationships as wives and husbands (5:22–33), children and parents (6:1–4), and slaves and masters (6:5–9) are to be transformed by the love of Christ. Paul goes on to say that they are to stand firm in the spiritual warfare and use the weapons of truth, righteousness, peace, faith, salvation, the Word of God, and prayer (6:10–20).

READING OF EPHESIANS 5

Prayer:

Lord, I want to imitate You as Your beloved child, and walk in love, just as Christ also loved me and gave Himself up for me, an offering and a sacrifice to God as a fragrant aroma.

MEDITATION PASSAGE FOR TODAY:

verses 1–2, 8–9, 15–21

P aul's important expression "in Christ" and its equivalent ("in Him") appear more often in Ephesians (35 times) than in any other New Testament book. The "in Christ" relationship that is available to every believer is rich and multifaceted: we have received every spiritual blessing in Christ (1:3); we were chosen in Christ (1:4, 11); we were adopted as God's children in Christ (1:5); we have redemption in Christ (1:7); our hope is in Christ (1:12); we were sealed in Christ (1:13); we were made alive in Christ (2:5); we were raised up with Christ and seated with Him in the heavenly realms (2:6); we are God's workmanship, created in Christ Jesus to do good works (2:10); we are joined together in Christ (2:21); we are sharers together in the promise in Christ Jesus (3:6); we can approach God with freedom and confidence in Christ (3:12); and we are called to strengthen ourselves in Christ's mighty power (6:10).

READING OF EPHESIANS 6

Prayer:

Lord, may I live in dependence upon Your strength and put on the full armor of God, so that I will be able to stand firm against the schemes of the devil.

MEDITATION PASSAGE FOR TODAY:

verses 10–13

P hilippians is an epistle of joy and encouragement that inspires its readers to focus their thoughts and actions on the pursuit of Christ. When our joy is threatened by adverse circumstances (chapter 1), disunity among people (chapter 2), the quest for accomplishments (chapter 3), or anxiety (chapter 4), this letter is a powerful tool that can help us get our eyes back on Jesus. Only by pursuing Jesus first will we discover the peace and contentment that comes from God.

Paul begins this epistle with a word of thanksgiving for the Philippians and a prayer for their spiritual growth in love and discernment (1:1–11). He then tells him about his imprisonment, the progress of the gospel, and his openness to either outcome (exoneration or execution) in his trial (1:12–26). This chapter concludes with an exhortation to contend for the gospel in the face of persecution (1:27–30).

READING OF PHILIPPIANS 1

Prayer:

Lord, may my love abound more and more in real knowledge and all discernment, so that I may approve the things that are excellent in order to be sincere and blameless until the day of Christ.

MEDITATION PASSAGE FOR TODAY:

verses 6, 9–11, 21

P aul exhorts his readers in Philippi to maintain a spirit of love and unity by pursuing the mind of Christ Jesus who served others through His incarnation and death (2:1–11). He calls them to cultivate this attitude (2:12–18), and illustrates it through the sacrificial service of Timothy and Epaphroditus (2:19–30).

While Philippians contains little doctrinal teaching, Paul's use of Christ's self-emptying in 2:5–11 as a model of other-centered humility is one of the most significant passages on the Person and work of Christ in the Bible. This is known as the *kenosis* passage from the Greek word that speaks of the empty-ing that was involved in the incarnation; Christ did not empty Himself of His deity, but divested Himself of the full manifesta-tion of His divine rights and attributes during His earthly life.

READING OF PHILIPPIANS 2

Prayer:

Lord, may I do nothing from selfishness or empty conceit, but with humility of mind may I regard others as more important than myself. May I have the attitude of Christ Jesus and look out for the interests of others.

MEDITATION PASSAGE FOR TODAY:

verses 3–13

Turning to the problem of legalistic influences, Paul refutes the attempt to attain righteousness through keeping the law by using his own life as an example of the futility of works-based righteousness (3:1–9). Having found true righteousness through faith in Christ, he presses on toward the goal of the upward call of God in Christ Jesus (3:10–16). He warns about those who set their mind on earthly things and contrasts this with his passion for heavenly things (3:17–21).

Because of its informality, Philippians does not follow an outline, but quickly moves through a variety of topics. The words "joy" and "rejoice" appear 16 times, words capturing the spirit of this epistle; Paul learned the secret of being content in any and every situation (4:12). His single-minded pursuit of the personal knowledge of Christ (3:10) and understanding that to live is Christ and to die is gain (1:21) are at the core of his being.

READING OF PHILIPPIANS 3

Prayer:

Lord, I lay hold of the righteousness which comes through faith in Christ Jesus. May I know Him and the power of His resurrection and the fellowship of His sufferings.

MEDITATION PASSAGE FOR TODAY:

verses 3, 8–14, 20–21

I n the last chapter, Paul exhorts the believers in Philippi to maintain unity, to enjoy God's peace by offering all anxieties to God in prayer, and to be content in their circumstances (4:1–13). After thanking them for participating in his ministry though their support, he closes with greetings and a benediction (4:14–23).

Paul wrote this letter to thank the Philippians for their gift, to convey his warm affection for them, and to encourage them to "[stand] firm in one spirit, with one mind striving together for the faith of the gospel" (1:27). He argues that joy springs out of unity, and that unity springs out of humility; the ultimate example of humility is the obedience of Christ Jesus to His Father's will (2:5–11).

READING OF PHILIPPIANS 4

Prayer:

Lord, may I be anxious for nothing, but in everything by prayer and supplication with thanksgiving, may I make my requests known to You. In this way, Your peace, which surpasses all comprehension, will guard my heart and mind in Christ Jesus.

MEDITATION PASSAGE FOR TODAY:

verses 4–9, 13, 19

C olossians may be the most Christ-centered book in Scripture—everything in it lifts the mind and heart to "the things above, where Christ is, seated at the right hand of God" (3:1). This epistle edifies the mind as it portrays the supremacy and Person of Christ, and it edifies the heart as it encourages us to pursue Him in our conduct and character.

After a brief greeting, Paul thanks God for the Colossians (1:3–8) and prays that they would come to a deeper knowledge and growth in Christ (1:9–14). He develops his theme of the supremacy of Jesus Christ by demonstrating Christ's pre-eminence in the realms of creation (1:15–18) and of redemption (1:19–2:3).

READING OF COLOSSIANS 1

Prayer:

Lord, I ask that I may be filled with the knowledge of Your will in all spiritual wisdom and understanding, so that I will walk in a manner worthy of You, to please You in all respects, bearing fruit in every good work and increasing in the knowledge of God.

MEDITATION PASSAGE FOR TODAY:

verses 9–20

H aving presented the preeminence of Christ in creation and redemption, Paul goes on to refute the false teachings of those who were promoting deceptive philosophy, legalistic regulations, misguided mysticism, and vain asceticism (2:4–23).

Paul wrote this Christ-centered epistle to combat the erroneous teachings that were beginning to take hold in Colossae, knowing that the best way to refute error is to focus on a clear presentation of the truth. He argues that Christ alone is sufficient for all things, and that the ascetic regulations, hidden knowledge, and mystical visions that were being promoted by the false teachers in Colossae were not only inadequate, but heretical. Christ holds all the treasures of wisdom and knowledge (2:3), so it is unnecessary to turn to spurious sources to find what He alone can offer.

READING OF COLOSSIANS 2

Prayer:

Lord, all the treasures of wisdom and knowledge are hidden in Christ, and in Him all the fullness of Deity dwells in bodily form. Just as I have received Him by faith, so may I walk in Him.

MEDITATION PASSAGE FOR TODAY:

verses 3, 6–10, 13–14

While the first half of Colossians presents the Person, character, and supremacy of Christ, the second half turns to the believer's pursuit of Christ through submission to Him and godly conduct in each area of life. Because of our union with Christ (3:1–4), we are to put the sinful manifestations of the old self to death (3:5–11) and demonstrate the life of the new self in Christ (3:12–17). This inward transformation should be expressed in the transformation of outward relationships in the family, in the marketplace, and in proclamation to unbelievers (3:18–4:6).

Paul urged his readers to keep their hope fixed on Christ alone. As they grow in this hope, it will be manifested in a quality of holiness in their relationships with others that is not based on rules and regulations, but on a growing personal relationship with Christ Jesus.

READING OF COLOSSIANS 3

Prayer:

Lord, when Christ, who is my life, is revealed, then I also will be revealed with Him in glory. Whatever I do in word or deed, may I do in the name of the Lord Jesus, giving thanks through Him to You.

MEDITATION PASSAGE FOR TODAY:

verses 1–4, 9–17

C hrist is the image of the invisible God by whom and for whom all things were created (1:15–16). In Him, all the fullness of the Deity dwells in bodily form (1:15, 19; 2:9), and He sustains the entire cosmos (1:16–17). Paul redefines the terms used by the Colossian heretics by arguing that only in Christ can one discover the true *gnosis* (knowledge) and *pleroma* (fullness); in Him are hidden "all the treasures of wisdom and knowledge" (2:3). He is the source of redemption and reconciliation to God (1:14, 20–22; 2:11–15), and He is the all-sufficient Savior of those who know Him (1:28; 2:10; 3:1–4). Christ is the "head of the body, the church; and He is the beginning, the first-born from the dead, so that He Himself will come to have first place in everything" (1:18).

READING OF COLOSSIANS 4

Prayer:

Lord, may I conduct myself with wisdom toward outsiders, making the most of the opportunity. May my speech always be with grace, so that I will know how I should respond to each person.

MEDITATION PASSAGE FOR TODAY:

verses 2–6

This warm and personal epistle encourages us to remain steadfast in our faith and to grow in sanctification. It gives us a model for relational ministry as Paul describes the way he worked with and nurtured the Thessalonians. It also exemplifies the kind of personal concern we should adopt for those we have been privileged to serve. This letter contains critical insights on the coming of the Lord for His saints and the nature of "the day of the Lord."

Paul begins this epistle of personal reflection, exhortation, encouragement, and instruction by giving thanks in light of the report he had received from Timothy about their work produced by faith, their labor prompted by love, and their endurance inspired by hope in Christ (1:1–3). He rejoices that their faith has inspired all the believers in Macedonia and Achaia (1:4–10).

READING OF 1 THESSALONIANS 1

Prayer:

Lord, You have called me to serve You, the living and true God, and to wait for Your Son from heaven, whom You raised from the dead, and who rescues us from the wrath to come.

MEDITATION PASSAGE FOR TODAY:

verses 3–5, 9–10

P aul's word of thanksgiving for the Thessalonians is followed by a review of his ministry in their midst and a defense of his care, concern, motives, and message (2:1–16).

First Thessalonians centers on the theme of the salvation and spiritual growth of the believers in Thessalonica. After hearing Timothy's report about the steadfastness of the Thessalonians' faith, Paul wrote this epistle to tell them how thankful he was for the reality of their growing faith and love in the face of persecution. He also responded to the false accusations of the Jewish opposition by reminding his readers of the selfless way he ministered to them and the truthfulness of the message he imparted to them.

READING OF 1 THESSALONIANS 2

Prayer:

Lord, may I love and serve others out of tenderness and affection as I encourage them to walk in a manner worthy of the God who calls us to His own kingdom and glory.

MEDITATION PASSAGE FOR TODAY:

verses 7–8, 13, 19–20

P aul explains that he was concerned after his departure
from the Thessalonians about their spiritual condition and
expresses his profound encouragement to hear that their faith
and love were continuing to grow (2:17–3:10). Before moving on
to a series of exhortations and instructions, Paul pauses to pray
for their continued spiritual progress (3:11–13).

This personal letter has much in common with 2 Corinthians; in both letters Paul defends his message and character in
view of slanderous opposition. In his defense of his ministry,
Paul reveals his motives, his compassion, his dedication, his
tenderness, and his concern for the people God had called him
to serve.

READING OF 1 THESSALONIANS 3

Prayer:

*Lord, I ask that You would cause us to increase and abound in
our love for one another, so that You may establish our hearts
without blame in holiness before You at the coming of our Lord
Jesus Christ with all His saints.*

MEDITATION PASSAGE FOR TODAY:

verses 9–13

P aul's practical exhortations begin with a reminder of his teaching on sexual purity, brotherly love, and personal responsibility (4:1–12). In answer to their concern about the destiny of believers who have died in Christ, the apostle comforts them with the hope of resurrection and reunion in Christ at His coming (4:13–18).

Christ is seen in this epistle as the Lord who will return from heaven and rescue His people from the coming wrath (1:10; 5:4–11). The certainty of His coming is a great source of hope for those who trust in Him, because both the dead in Christ and those who are alive when He comes will be resurrected and united in Him (4:13–18). He will sanctify (3:13; 5:23) and reward (2:19–20) all who hope in Him.

READING OF 1 THESSALONIANS 4

Prayer:

Lord, I thank You for the blessed hope of being caught up to meet the Lord Jesus in the air when He descends from heaven to receive us to Himself.

MEDITATION PASSAGE FOR TODAY:

verses 13–18

P aul continues with a discourse on the future day of the Lord
and exhorts the Thessalonians to be alert and self-controlled
as children of the light whose destiny is to live together with
Christ (5:1–11). The epistle ends with specific admonitions and
instructions that relate to their sanctification (5:12–22) and with
a benediction and parting thoughts (5:23–28).

Both of Paul's Thessalonian epistles deal with matters of
eschatology (prophecy), and all five chapters of First Thessalonians refer to the return of Christ (1:10; 2:19; 3:13; 4:13–18;
5:1–11, 23) with very vivid and practical prophetic material in
4:13–5:11. This is one of the most important biblical passages
concerning the coming of Christ.

READING OF 1 THESSALONIANS 5

Prayer:

*Lord, may I rejoice always, pray without ceasing, and in every-
thing give thanks; for this is Your will for me in Christ Jesus.*

MEDITATION PASSAGE FOR TODAY:

verses 8–11, 16–18, 23

The truth of Paul's teaching in his first epistle to the Thessalonians was distorted by false teachers who claimed that the day of the Lord was already taking place. This distortion led in turn to a mentality of passivity and idleness. This corrective epistle is of great value in clarifying the biblical teaching concerning the coming day of the Lord, as well as promoting a balance between waiting and working.

The letter begins with a salutation (1:1–2) and a word of thanksgiving for the growing faith and perseverance of the believers in Thessalonica in the face of mounting opposition (1:3–4). Paul encourages them to endure, knowing that their sufferings will be repaid and that God will deal in righteousness with those who have been oppressing them (1:5–10). The first chapter ends with a prayer that God will fulfill His good purposes in their lives (1:11–13).

READING OF 2 THESSALONIANS 1

Prayer:

Lord, I ask that You will count me worthy of Your calling, and fulfill every desire for goodness and the work of faith with power, so that the name of the Lord Jesus will be glorified.

MEDITATION PASSAGE FOR TODAY:

verses 11–12

I n view of some prophecy or a report falsely attributed to Paul, the church was being disturbed by the deception that the day of the Lord (1 Thessalonians 5:1–11) had come. Paul shows that this cannot be so until the man of lawlessness is revealed and the one who holds him back is taken out of the way (2:1–12). Paul adds a word of encouragement, exhorts his readers to stand firm, and prays for them (2:13–17).

The first two chapters of 2 Thessalonians focus on the return of Christ and teach that when He is "revealed from heaven with His mighty angels in flaming fire," those who do not know God and do not obey the gospel of our Lord Jesus will be judged (1:6–10). But Christ will not judge the earth until the "apostasy comes first, and the man of lawlessness is revealed" (2:3, 6–12). Thus, Paul's teaching on the second coming is a comfort for believers and a warning to unbelievers.

READING OF 2 THESSALONIANS 2

Prayer:

Lord, may our Lord Jesus Christ Himself and God our Father, who has loved us and given us eternal comfort and good hope by grace, comfort and strengthen our hearts in every good work and word.

MEDITATION PASSAGE FOR TODAY:

verses 13–14, 16–17

A fter a request for prayer on his behalf (3:1–5), Paul admonishes those among the Thessalonians who have become idle and are living off the resources of others rather than earning their own provisions (3:6–15). The doctrine of the return of Christ should stimulate responsible living rather than indolence. This brief epistle concludes with a benediction and greetings (3:16–18).

The theme of 2 Thessalonians is comfort and correction in view of practical and doctrinal obstacles to spiritual maturity. Those who followed Jesus in Thessalonica needed to know that their persecution would be vindicated at the return of Christ, that the day of the Lord was yet future, and that they should continue to be diligent rather than undisciplined while they awaited the coming of the Lord.

READING OF 2 THESSALONIANS 3

Prayer:

Lord, I ask that You would direct my heart into the love of God and into the steadfastness of Christ.

MEDITATION PASSAGE FOR TODAY:

verses 3, 5, 13

First Timothy is full of specific principles of leadership and holy living, and it is particularly relevant to anyone who is in a position of spiritual influence. This is an extremely practical book that touches on issues of doctrine, public worship, the problem of false teaching, the treatment of various groups within the church, wealth, contentment, and personal integrity.

Paul begins this letter by warning his young associate about the problem of the misuse of the Law of Moses by false teachers (1:3–11). He looks back to his dramatic conversion to Christ and encourages Timothy to fulfill his own God-ordained purpose by fighting the good fight (1:12–20).

READING OF 1 TIMOTHY 1

Prayer:

Lord, You are the King eternal, immortal, invisible, the only God; to You be honor and glory forever and ever.

MEDITATION PASSAGE FOR TODAY:

verses 5, 14–17

Turning to matters of church worship and leadership, Paul stresses that the men of the church should be leaders in prayer (2:1–8) and that the women should be characterized by inner godliness (2:9–15).

First Timothy is a personal letter, but it is written in an authoritative and exhortative tone because of the specific problems it addresses in light of Timothy's leadership responsibilities during Paul's absence from Ephesus. Since it was written to his trusted and personal associate, it refers to doctrine without developing it and encourages Timothy to stand firm in the truth. This epistle contains the clearest and most explicit directions for the organization and administration of the church in the Bible.

READING OF 1 TIMOTHY 2

Prayer:

Lord, I acknowledge that there is one God, and one mediator also between God and men, the man Christ Jesus, who gave Himself as a ransom for all, the testimony given at the proper time.

MEDITATION PASSAGE FOR TODAY:

verses 1–6

P aul's purpose in writing this epistle to his disciple and em-
issary, Timothy, is clear in 3:15: "in case I am delayed, I
write so that you will know how one ought to conduct himself
in the household of God, which is the church of the living God,
the pillar and support of the truth." This letter is really a leadership manual that was designed to provide practical guidance
to Timothy on a number of specific issues, including personal
exhortations to godliness and development of his spiritual gifts,
directions for worship in the churches, defending apostolic doctrine in the face of false teaching, instructions about widows
and elders, the temptations of wealth, and faithfulness to his
calling.

Paul lists the qualifications for overseers in 3:1–7 (in the New
Testament church, bishops and elders referred to the same office; Acts 20:17, 28; Titus 1:5, 7), and the qualifications for deacons in 3:8–13.

READING OF 1 TIMOTHY 3

Prayer:

Lord, by common confession, great is the mystery of godliness:
He who was revealed in the flesh, was vindicated in the Spirit,
seen by angels, proclaimed among the nations, believed on in
the world, taken up in glory.

MEDITATION PASSAGE FOR TODAY:

verse 16

T he epistles of 1 and 2 Timothy and Titus do not fit against the background of the book of Acts since they were written after Paul's release from his first Roman imprisonment (Acts 28). The events in the last years of Paul's life must be reconstructed from clues that are provided in these epistles. It appears that in spite of his statement in Acts 20:25, Paul did return to Ephesus, and after Timothy joined him there, he instructed Timothy to stay in Ephesus while he went into Macedonia (1:3). He wrote this epistle to Timothy while in Macedonia (probably Philippi) in A.D. 62 or 63 when he realized his return to Ephesus might be delayed (3:14–15).

In view of the influence of false teachers, Paul exhorts Timothy to counter error with the truths of the gospel and to set an example to others of purity of life and doctrine as he continues to use his spiritual gift (4:1–16).

READING OF 1 TIMOTHY 4

Prayer:

Lord, may I hold fast to the truth and discipline myself for the purpose of godliness as I fix my hope on You, the living God.

MEDITATION PASSAGE FOR TODAY:

verses 4–5

P aul's two letters to Timothy and his letter to Titus are collectively known as the Pastoral Epistles because they deal
with issues of shepherding and oversight of local churches. In
this chapter, Paul gives his associate Timothy specific instructions on how the church should provide for widows and for the
elders who direct the affairs of the church (5:1–25).

First Timothy presents Christ Jesus as the one mediator between God and humanity who gave Himself as a ransom for all
(2:5–6). Christ Jesus came into the world to save sinners, and
He is "the Savior of all men, especially of believers" (1:15; 4:10).
It is in Him that strength, mercy, faith, love, salvation, hope,
godliness, and contentment (1:12–14; 2:3–6; 4:10; 6:6) are to be
found.

READING OF 1 TIMOTHY 5

Prayer:

*Lord, may I do nothing in a spirit of partiality. I ask for Your
power to show love, patience, kindness, and goodness to each
person I encounter.*

MEDITATION PASSAGE FOR TODAY:

verses 21, 24–25

After a word concerning those who are slaves (6:1–2), Paul condemns the false teaching that godliness is a means to financial gain, affirming instead that contentment is more valuable than material abundance (6:3–10). He concludes this epistle with a charge to Timothy to endure in the good fight of the faith (6:11–16) and a final word about those who are rich in this present world (6:17–21).

The Pastoral Epistles were Paul's only recorded letters to individuals (his letter to Philemon was addressed to several people). As the last of Paul's letters in Scripture, 1 Timothy and Titus were written after his first imprisonment, and 2 Timothy was written during his second imprisonment near the end of his life.

READING OF 1 TIMOTHY 6

Prayer:

Lord, You are the blessed and only Sovereign, the King of kings and Lord of lords, who alone possesses immortality and dwells in unapproachable light, whom no man has seen or can see. To You be honor and eternal dominion!

MEDITATION PASSAGE FOR TODAY:

verses 6–16

S econd Timothy contains Paul's parting words to his younger associate, Timothy. By listening in, we can gain wise and godly counsel that is as relevant to the problems we face today as it was to the problems Timothy faced in the first century. This is a powerful manual for spiritual combat that encourages us to be diligent and courageous and to make the most of the opportunities that God has given us.

After a brief greeting, Paul reviews Timothy's conversion, then he reminds him to fan into flame the gift he received and to overcome timidity with God's power (1:1–7). He invites Timothy to join with him in suffering for the gospel, knowing that Christ will guard whatever He entrusts to him (1:8–14). Paul commends Onesiphorus who supported him and sought him out in Rome when other believers abandoned him (1:15–18).

READING OF 2 TIMOTHY 1

Prayer:

Lord, I know whom I have believed and I am convinced that He is able to guard what I have entrusted to Him until the day of Christ Jesus.

MEDITATION PASSAGE FOR TODAY:

verses 7–12

P aul encourages his younger associate Timothy to engage in a ministry of reproducing the life of Christ in others and of equipping them to do the same. He uses the metaphors of a soldier, an athlete, and a farmer to convey the need for diligence in discipleship (2:1–13). He admonishes Timothy to be strong in the word of truth and to avoid godless chatter, youthful lusts, and fruitless quarrels (2:14–26).

Those who wish to be active and effective in the Lord's service should call on the Lord out of a pure heart. If we pray for the eyes to see what God is doing in our lives, we will realize we have more ministry opportunities than we thought.

READING OF 2 TIMOTHY 2

Prayer:

Lord, I want to be a vessel for honor, sanctified and useful for the Master, prepared for every good work. By Your grace and power, I want to participate in Your eternal plan. Open my eyes to the opportunities You give me to love and serve others with eternal values at heart.

MEDITATION PASSAGE FOR TODAY:

verses 1–2, 10–13, 22

P aul predicts a time of increasing arrogance, rebelliousness, and vulnerability to spiritual deception (3:1–9), warning Timothy that he can expect that persecution for the sake of following Christ will increase (3:10–13). He reminds Timothy to stay strong in Scripture and to use it effectively in this spiritual combat (3:14–17).

Paul's letters to his disciple indicate that Timothy was youthful, frequently ill, and timid (1 Timothy 4:12; 5:23; 2 Timothy 1:7), but that he was a trustworthy and gifted teacher. The apostle wrote this letter to encourage him to be faithful to his calling and to stand firm in the face of obstacles to the spreading of the gospel. Because Timothy was encountering a number of hardships, Paul wanted to strengthen him to handle external persecution and internal problems of false doctrine and dissension within the churches. This was especially urgent in light of the fact that Paul was nearing the end of his ministry and needed to entrust important areas into the care of his faithful associate and disciple.

READING OF 2 TIMOTHY 3

Prayer:

Lord, I acknowledge that all Scripture is God-breathed and profitable for teaching, for reproof, for correction, for training in righteousness, so that we may be adequate, equipped for every good work.

MEDITATION PASSAGE FOR TODAY:

verses 12, 15–17

I n his final exhortation, Paul charges his associate to preach and teach the Word, to correct, rebuke, encourage, endure hardship, and do the work of an evangelist (4:1–5). Paul concludes this epistle with thoughts about his future reward with Christ and with personal remarks and requests (4:6–22).

As Paul's last recorded epistle (written during his second Roman imprisonment in A.D. 67), 2 Timothy serves as his final testament to the world. He reviews Christ's faithfulness in his past and commissions Timothy to carry on the good work of proclaiming Christ in the present. Paul also looks ahead to the future when he will be rewarded with the crown of righteousness after being brought safely to the Lord's heavenly kingdom.

READING OF 2 TIMOTHY 4

Prayer:

Lord, by Your grace, may I be able to say at the end of my earthly sojourn, "I have fought the good fight, I have finished the course, I have kept the faith."

MEDITATION PASSAGE FOR TODAY:

verses 1–2, 5, 7–8, 18

T his epistle is a concise manual of conduct for assemblies of brothers and sisters in Christ. Titus 1 and 1 Timothy 3 are critical to the organization of the local church because they outline God's requirements for the leadership of the body of believers. The letter to Titus provides us with instruction on the ordination of elders, dealing with false teachers, the roles of different groups within the church, and the relationship between sound doctrine and godly behavior.

Paul's salutation to Titus contains a rich statement of God's redemptive purpose for His people (1:1–4). Paul then launches into the principal purpose of the letter, which is to provide instructions for the oversight and conduct of the churches in Crete. Paul gives his associate a list of qualifications to assist him in discerning the right people for this leadership office in each church (1:5–9) then warns him about the problem of corruption and false teaching (1:10–16).

READING OF TITUS 1

Prayer:

Lord, may I be a servant of Your truth and hold fast the faithful word not only in my thinking, but also in my daily practice.

MEDITATION PASSAGE FOR TODAY:

verses 1–3

Paul gives Titus clear directives concerning the way each group (older men, older women, younger women, young men, and slaves) in the assemblies should conduct themselves (2:1–10). This is followed by a concise affirmation of the hope and transforming power of the gospel of Christ (2:11–15).

Titus presents Christ as the supreme manifestation of the grace, mercy, and redemptive purposes of God. It is by His grace that we are justified, and through Him we have become heirs who enjoy the hope of eternal life. This hope is in "the appearing of the glory of our great God and Savior, Christ Jesus" (2:13).

READING OF TITUS 2

Prayer:

Lord, may I deny ungodliness and worldly desires and live sensibly, righteously and godly in the present age, looking for the blessed hope and the appearing of the glory of our great God and Savior, Christ Jesus.

MEDITATION PASSAGE FOR TODAY:

verses 11–14

After an exhortation concerning the general conduct of all believers (3:1–2), Paul gives a sublime summary of how the kindness, love, and mercy of God brought about our salvation through grace and not by works (3:3–7). But good works should follow from this redemption (3:8). This letter closes with instructions on dealing with divisive people (3:9–11) and some final remarks (3:12–15).

Paul wrote this epistle to follow through on his instructions for the appointment of elders in every city in Crete by giving Titus a list of qualifications to use in this process (1:5–9; cf. 1 Timothy 3). He emphasizes the need for sound doctrine by providing three important summaries of the faith (1:1–3; 2:11–14; 3:3–7).

READING OF TITUS 3

Prayer:

Lord, You saved us, not on the basis of deeds which we have done in righteousness, but according to Your mercy, by the washing of regeneration and renewing by the Holy Spirit, whom You poured out upon us richly through Jesus Christ our Savior, so that being justified by His grace, we would be made heirs according to the hope of eternal life.

MEDITATION PASSAGE FOR TODAY:

verses 3–7

P aul's purpose in writing this letter was to appeal to Philemon on behalf of a man who was previously a useless slave, a thief, and a runaway. Because of Onesimus' conversion to faith in Christ, Paul argues that his character has been transformed and that he should be moved from bondage to brotherhood in the eyes of his former master. Just as Philemon himself received grace and forgiveness in Christ, so he must extend the same to this new brother in the Lord. Paul urges Philemon to receive Onesimus just as he would receive him and even invites Philemon to charge Onesimus' debt to him.

Philemon is a brief but powerful testimony to the transforming power of faith, forgiveness, and freedom in Christ. This transformation on the vertical level should result in transformation on the horizontal level of our relationships with others. This epistle teaches us that spiritual change produces social change.

READING OF PHILEMON

Prayer:

Lord, may I no longer view people according to the flesh, but according to the way You see them, as people You love and for whom Christ gave His life.

MEDITATION PASSAGE FOR TODAY:

verses 6, 15–18

H ebrews is a profound and powerful book that uses a wide variety of Old Testament passages to present a clear case for the superiority of Christ over everything that preceded Him. This book adds immeasurably to our understanding of His Person and work and applies this understanding to the dynamics of spiritual growth in the life of the believer. Hebrews 11 is one of the most extraordinary chapters in Scripture, the clearest exposition of the meaning and rewards of faith in the Bible.

Hebrews immediately launches into its theme of the superiority of the Person and work of Jesus Christ by showing that He is the supreme revelation of God (1:1-3). Because He is worshipped by the angels, He is superior to them (1:4-14).

READING OF HEBREWS 1

Prayer:

Lord, I confess that Your Son is the radiance of Your glory and the exact representation of Your nature upholding all things by the word of His power.

MEDITATION PASSAGE FOR TODAY:

verses 1-4, 14

Hebrews contrasts the temporary Aaronic priesthood with the High Priesthood of Christ in the order of Melchizedek. He is equally divine (1:1–3, 8) and human (2:9, 14, 17–18), and He fulfills the three orders of prophet, priest, and king. His perfect and voluntary sacrifice is the fulfillment of all that was anticipated but not realized in the involuntary animal sacrifices of the Old Testament. Unlike those sacrifices, His never needs to be repeated. Through His incarnation, Jesus understands the human condition: He became the author of our salvation and our merciful and faithful high priest. "For since He Himself was tempted in that which He has suffered, He is able to come to the aid of those who are tempted."

READING OF HEBREWS 2

Prayer:

Lord, I give You thanks that Your Son partook of flesh and blood, that through death He might render powerless him who had the power of death, that is, the devil, and might free those who through fear of death were subject to slavery all their lives.

MEDITATION PASSAGE FOR TODAY:

verses 9–10, 14–18

The author of Hebrews argues that Jesus is superior to Moses, since Moses was a servant while Christ is the Son (3:1–6). Thus, this book warns of the danger of unbelief and rebellion against Him (3:7–19). Christ offers a better rest than Joshua, since this rest is appropriated by faith in Him (4:1–13). As our great high priest in the order of Melchizedek, Christ is able to identify with the human condition because He suffered and "became to all those who obey Him the source of eternal salvation" (4:14–5:10).

Since Jesus was tempted in all things as we are, but without sin, He can sympathize with our weaknesses and we can "draw near with confidence to the throne of grace, so that we may receive mercy and find grace to help in time of need."

READING OF HEBREWS 4

Prayer:

Lord, Your word is living and active and sharper than any two-edged sword, piercing as far as the division of soul and spirit, of both joints and marrow, and able to judge the thoughts and intentions of the heart.

MEDITATION PASSAGE FOR TODAY:

verses 2, 12–16

The author urges his readers not to fall away but to press on to spiritual maturity and to put their hope in God's promises (5:11–6:20). Christ's priesthood is superior to that of the Levites (7:1–28); as such, He is the mediator of a better covenant than the Mosaic covenant (8:1–13).

The author of Hebrews skillfully uses a great range of Old Testament quotations and allusions to build a careful case for the finality of Christ's priestly sacrifice. The rich doctrinal contributions of this book include its emphasis on the present priestly ministry of Christ, its development of the atonement of Christ, and its contrast between both the old and new covenants and between the earthly and heavenly sanctuaries. Hebrews sheds a great deal of light on the typology of the Mosaic Law and the offerings and feasts in Leviticus.

READING OF HEBREWS 8

Prayer:

Lord, I give thanks for Jesus our high priest, who has taken His seat at the right hand of the throne of the Majesty in the heavens as the mediator of the new covenant.

MEDITATION PASSAGE FOR TODAY:

verses 1–2, 6

As our high priest, Jesus ministers in a better, heavenly, tabernacle, and His blood sacrifice is superior to the sacrifices offered in the earthly sanctuary (9:1–10:18).

Hebrews builds a cumulative argument to demonstrate the superiority of Christ over the old covenant, priesthood, and sacrifices. This theme is developed in the frequent use of the word "better" or "superior" as well as the use of the terms "heavenly" and "perfect" to describe the greatness of Christ's Person and work in comparison to what was previously revealed. He is better than the angels in that they worship Him; He is better than Moses in that He created him; He offers a better rest than Joshua, a better priesthood than Levi, a better covenant, a better sanctuary, and a better sacrifice; He also provides the power to live a better life.

READING OF HEBREWS 9

Prayer:

Lord, it is the blood of Christ, who through the eternal Spirit offered Himself without blemish to God, which cleanses my conscience from dead works to serve the living God.

MEDITATION PASSAGE FOR TODAY:

verses 11–15, 27–28

B ecause of the manifold superiority of Christ Jesus, the author of this epistle calls his readers to conduct themselves in obedience to Jesus and to persevere in their sufferings for His sake (10:19–39). Like the obedient men and women of the Old Testament, their faith must be in God's character, and their hope must be in His promised heavenly rewards (11:1–40).

Since "faith is the assurance of things hoped for, the conviction of things not seen," we must acknowledge with the men and women who are listed in this chapter that we will not receive the fulfillment of God's promises in this life, but that we await "a better country, that is, a heavenly one."

READING OF HEBREWS 11

Prayer:

Lord, it is by faith that I understand that the worlds were prepared by Your word, so that what is seen was not made out of things which are visible. And without faith it is impossible to please You, for whoever comes to You must believe that You are and that You are a rewarder of those who seek You.

MEDITATION PASSAGE FOR TODAY:

verses 1, 3, 6, 13, 16, 39–40

I n this chapter, the readers of this epistle are encouraged to endure hardship and discipline for the sake of holiness, and they are warned not to refuse God during these difficult times.

The purpose for the careful exposition in Hebrews of the superiority of Christ's Person, priesthood, covenant, sanctuary, and sacrifice is to show the folly of moving away from the substance back to the shadow. The author sought to exhort his readers not to revert back to Judaism and to encourage them to go on to maturity in Christ. As "strangers and exiles on the earth" (11:13), they must realize that their sufferings for Christ are part of God's purpose, and that their heavenly Father disciplines them for their good, so that they may share His holiness.

READING OF HEBREWS 12

Prayer:

Lord, may I lay aside every encumbrance and the sin which so easily entangles me, and may I run with endurance the race that is set before me, fixing my eyes on Jesus, the author and perfecter of faith, who for the joy set before Him endured the cross, despising the shame, and has sat down at the right hand of the throne of God.

MEDITATION PASSAGE FOR TODAY:

verses 1–3, 11, 22–24, 28–29

The letter to the Hebrews concludes with a series of exhortations to purity, contentment, Christlike character, service, and submission (13:1–17) as well as personal instructions and a beautiful benediction (13:18–25).

Hebrews is the only New Testament book whose authorship remains a mystery. Despite its anonymity, its spiritual quality and depth overcame early questions about its inclusion in the New Testament canon. The original readers clearly knew the author (13:18–24) who was an associate of Timothy, but there is no consistent tradition as to his identity. Some in the early church attributed it to Paul, others to Barnabas, to Luke, and to Clement. There are indeed some similarities in the style and content of Hebrews and the Pauline epistles, but there are also enough dissimilarities to lead the majority of New Testament scholars to reject the Pauline authorship theory. Suggestions in modern scholarship include Apollos, Silas (Silvanus), Luke, Philip, and Clement of Rome, but no one knows.

READING OF HEBREWS 13

Prayer:

Lord, You are the God of peace who brought up from the dead the great Shepherd of the sheep through the blood of the eternal covenant, even Jesus our Lord. May You equip us in every good thing to do Your will, working in us that which is pleasing in Your sight, through Jesus Christ, to whom be the glory forever and ever.

MEDITATION PASSAGE FOR TODAY:

verses 1–8, 14–16, 20–21

J ames is a powerful and practical manual on the application of faith in Christ to the struggles and relationships we encounter every day. With force and clarity, this epistle relates Christlike conduct to a wide range of topics, making it always convicting to read. James maps the behavior of belief and shows how faith perseveres under trials, resists temptations, responds to Scripture, overcomes favoritism, leads to good works, controls the tongue, produces wisdom, submits to God, resists the lures of the world and the devil, depends on God and not on riches, waits patiently for Christ's coming, and results in answered prayer.

After a brief greeting (1:1) James speaks of the eternal perspective believers need to cultivate when they are facing trials so that they will be able to persevere when tested and tempted (1:2–18). They must not only listen to the word, but apply it to their actions (1:19–27).

READING OF JAMES 1

Prayer:

Lord, every good thing given and every perfect gift is from above, coming down from the Father of lights, with whom there is no variation or shifting shadow.

MEDITATION PASSAGE FOR TODAY:

verses 2–5, 12, 17–22

T urning to the problem of the preferential treatment of the wealthy, James instructs his readers to love the poor and the rich alike (2:1–13). He contrasts profession of faith with possession of faith and argues that a genuine faith is expressed in deeds (2:14–26). While faith alone justifies us before God (Romans 4), it is only by the works of faith that we are justified before others (2:24).

James is addressed to "the twelve tribes who are dispersed abroad" (1:1), a phrase refering to the Hebrew Christians who resided outside of Palestine. These Jewish believers in Jesus the Messiah were encountering many trials and needed to be encouraged and exhorted to persevere in their faith. This epistle makes no mention of Gentile believers and appears to have been written around A.D. 46–49 before the Jerusalem council in Acts 15. According to Josephus, James was martyred in A.D. 62.

READING OF JAMES 2

Prayer:

Lord, may I not hold my faith in our glorious Lord Jesus Christ with an attitude of personal favoritism. May my faith in Him become evident to others through my works.

MEDITATION PASSAGE FOR TODAY:

verses 1, 12, 26

DAY 338—JAMES 3

The tongue is the hardest thing in nature to control; our speech can lead to blessing or cursing, to life or to death (3:1–12). James contrasts two kinds of wisdom, the heavenly and the earthly, and exhorts his readers to turn away from envy and selfish ambition to love, mercy, and peace (3:13–18).

This epistle is the primary wisdom literature of the New Testament, strongly influenced by the Book of Proverbs and the Sermon on the Mount. It combines the pithy maxims of the Proverbs with the fiery rhetoric of Amos in its relentlessly ethical stance. It is full of vivid imagery and sharp commands (there are 54 imperatives in its 108 verses). This is a very formal letter that differs from the Pauline epistles in that James says nothing at all about his personal circumstances. Because of its specific treatment of so many situations in life, James is the most practical book in the New Testament offering timeless principles which apply just as well to life today as they did in the first century.

READING OF JAMES 3

Prayer:

Lord, may I walk in the wisdom from above that is first pure, then peaceable, gentle, reasonable, full of mercy and good fruits, unwavering, without hypocrisy.

MEDITATION PASSAGE FOR TODAY:

verses 13–18

S elfishness and materialism lead to quarrels, disunity, and pride; James counsels us to humble ourselves and submit to God rather than envying and slandering others (4:1–12). Those who engage in business must submit their plans to God's will and avoid the arrogance of autonomy (4:13–17).

The theme of James is the character of true faith as it is expressed in various situations and relationships. The Jewish believers scattered throughout the Roman Empire were struggling with trials and temptations. There were evidently also problems in their assemblies with spiritual apathy, preferential treatment of the wealthy, disunity, and materialism that needed to be corrected. James wrote this letter to exhort them to persevere in obedience to the truth and to apply a living faith in Christ to their attitudes and actions. A lack of change in personal character and conduct is symptomatic of a dead faith.

READING OF JAMES 4

Prayer:

Lord, may I submit to You in all things and resist the devil. May I draw near to You and humble myself in Your presence.

MEDITATION PASSAGE FOR TODAY:

verses 4, 6–8, 17

Those who depend on their wealth and oppress others will meet with a day of reckoning (5:1–6). Those who are suffering and oppressed must persevere in hope of the promised coming of the Lord (5:7–12). This epistle concludes with a teaching on the healing and restoration that can be accomplished through the prayer offered in faith (5:13–20).

James calls himself "a bond-servant of God and of the Lord Jesus Christ" (1:1) and speaks of his readers as brethren whose faith is in "our glorious Lord Jesus Christ" (2:1). While he says less than other New Testament writers about the Person and work of Christ, his words are saturated with allusions to the teaching of our Lord (there are 15 indirect references in this epistle to the Sermon on the Mount). He anticipates the Lord's coming as the Judge in 5:7–9.

READING OF JAMES 5

Prayer:

Lord, may I order my steps in accordance with Your Word and live in anticipation of the coming of the Lord Jesus. May I be a person of prayer in all circumstances.

MEDITATION PASSAGE FOR TODAY:

verses 8, 11, 16

F irst Peter gives us a divine perspective on living as aliens and strangers in a world that is increasingly hostile to the gospel of Christ. Each of its five chapters alludes to suffering as a very real part of the Christian experience. This letter provides us with counsel and comfort in times of adversity and affliction by pointing us to the living hope we have in our relationship with Christ.

This epistle presents the grace of God in our *salvation* as the foundation for an attitude of *submission* in the context of *suffering* for Christ's sake. It begins with a portrait of salvation in terms of the believer's future hope of an imperishable inheritance (1:3–5), the joy that is available in spite of present trials (1:6–9), and the predictions of this salvation in the past (1:10–12).

READING OF 1 PETER 1

Prayer:

Lord, I bless You, the God and Father of our Lord Jesus Christ, who according to Your great mercy has caused us to be born again to a living hope through the resurrection of Jesus Christ from the dead, to obtain an imperishable inheritance.

MEDITATION PASSAGE FOR TODAY:

verses 3–5, 8–9, 13, 22–23

I n view of the gift of salvation, Peter urges believers to grow in holiness and to purify themselves in obedience to the truth (1:13–2:12). As "a chosen race, a royal priesthood, a holy nation, a people for God's own possession" (2:9), they should grow up in their salvation and manifest a new quality of life before a watching world. This gift of salvation is best expressed on a relational level by an attitude of submission and service to others (2:13–3:12). Believers should submit for the Lord's sake to those in government and to those who personally have authority over them (2:13–20). This attitude of submission to God's purposes is best illustrated in the undeserved suffering of Christ (2:21–25) who endured sinlessly, silently, and as a substitute for others.

READING OF 1 PETER 2

Prayer:

Lord, may I put aside all malice, deceit, hypocrisy, envy, and slander, and long for the pure milk of the word so that by it I may grow in respect to salvation.

MEDITATION PASSAGE FOR TODAY:

verses 1–3, 9, 24–25

P eter extends this theme of submission to the marital relationship (3:1–7) and to the pursuit of harmonious relationships with others (3:8–12). Because submission to the Lordship
of Christ may lead to suffering for His sake, Peter encourages
his readers to order their lives in such a way that those who
slander them will be ashamed (3:13–17). Peter also points to the
work of Christ in bringing about their salvation (3:18–22).

The resurrection transformed the life of Peter, resulting in
his playing a key role in the formation of the early church and
in the spread of the gospel from the Jews to both the Samaritans and the Gentiles. Peter apparently traveled extensively
and ministered in various Roman provinces (1 Corinthians 9:5).
According to tradition, he was crucified upside down in Rome
prior to the death of Nero in A.D. 68, probably sometime in
A.D. 64–66.

READING OF 1 PETER 3

Prayer:

*Lord, may I sanctify Christ as Lord in my heart, always be-
ing ready to make a defense to everyone who asks me to give
an account for the hope that is in me, yet with gentleness and
reverence.*

MEDITATION PASSAGE FOR TODAY:

verses 8–9, 15, 18

P eter urges his readers to live no longer in the lusts of the flesh, but in God's power and in service to one another (4:1–11). If they suffer for the sake of Christ, they should commit themselves to the Lord and continue in His service (4:12–19).

First Peter develops the theme of a biblical response to suffering in the lives of believers. Because Peter could anticipate a growing wave of persecution among those who follow Christ, it appears that he wrote this epistle not long before Christianity was declared to be an illegal religion. He wanted his readers to be prepared to persevere under adversity and not to be surprised at the painful trial they were suffering, as though something strange were happening to them (4:12). Instead, they should rejoice that they are participating in the sufferings of Christ, because they will exult at the revelation of His glory (4:13).

READING OF 1 PETER 4

Prayer:

Lord, may I be of sound judgment and sober spirit for the purpose of prayer, and may I remain fervent in my love for others.

MEDITATION PASSAGE FOR TODAY:

verses 7–13

P eter exhorts the elders to serve as examples to their flocks and encourages all his readers to pursue a lifestyle of humility and hope. He reminds his readers that their brethren throughout the world are also undergoing the same kind of sufferings (5:9), that they are not in a unique situation. Peter wanted to encourage them to submit to God and His loving purposes for their lives, to draw on His strength in the present while maintaining a clear hope of their heavenly future. Thus, the more they realize that they are strangers and aliens in the world, and that their true destiny and home is eternal glory in the presence of the Lord, the better they will be able to stand fast in the true grace of God (5:12).

READING OF 1 PETER 5

Prayer:

Lord, by Your grace may I clothe myself with humility toward others, and humble myself under Your mighty hand, that You may exalt me at the proper time.

MEDITATION PASSAGE FOR TODAY:

verses 5–11

While 1 Peter deals with the problem of external opposition to the gospel, 2 Peter confronts the even more insidious problem of internal opposition to the truth by teachers who profess to be believers but distort the gospel. These false teachers "secretly introduce destructive heresies" (2:1) even to the point of denying Christ, and their teachings seduce believers into error and immorality. This epistle tells us how to deal with the problem of false teaching, making it more relevant in our time of proliferating spiritual counterfeits than ever before.

After a brief salutation (1:1–2), Peter speaks of God's "precious and magnificent promises" and the consequent life of faith, moral excellence, knowledge, self-control, perseverance, godliness, brotherly kindness, and love which these promises should produce (1:3–11). Knowing that his martyrdom was imminent, Peter wanted to stir up his readers to remember and hold fast to the prophetic word (1:12–21).

READING OF 2 PETER 1

Prayer:

Lord, by Your grace may I grow in faith, moral excellence, knowledge, self-control, perseverance, godliness, brotherly kindness, and love.

MEDITATION PASSAGE FOR TODAY:

verses 3–4, 16–19

H aving affirmed true prophecy, Peter warns of the dangers of false teachers who deny the truths of the gospel and seek to captivate others (2:1–22). He not only denounces their teachings and conduct, but also anticipates the divine judgment they will receive.

In contrast to the external dangers of persecution of the Christian community in Asia Minor that Peter addressed in his first epistle, his second epistle confronts the internal dangers of false teachers that threatened to corrupt the body of believers in both doctrine and practice. The focus of 1 Peter is *suffering* for the sake of commitment to Christ, while the focus of 2 Peter is *knowledge* of the truth in a context of misleading errors. Peter's first epistle deals with the implications of spiritual *birth*, and his second epistle stresses the importance of spiritual *growth*.

READING OF 2 PETER 2

Prayer:

Lord, may I come to know the truth of Your revealed Word so well that I will be able to quickly discern and avoid the influence of false teaching.

MEDITATION PASSAGE FOR TODAY:

verses 1, 9

The promised coming of Christ will happen suddenly and certainly, and Peter refers back to the creation and the flood to refute the argument of scoffers who deny that the day of the Lord will arrive (3:1–10). In view of the fact that the earth and its works will be destroyed, Peter urges his readers to live holy and blameless lives as they look forward to a new heaven and a new earth (3:11–18).

Peter contrasts the destiny of those who are disseminating error and immorality with those who affirm the Scriptures and develop in Christlike character, and he exhorts his readers to "grow in the grace and knowledge of our Lord and Savior Jesus Christ" (3:18). Sanctification through application and conformity to Scriptural truth is the best defense against spiritual counterfeits. Peter wrote this epistle as a lasting reminder to remain faithful to the foundations of the faith and to urge believers to live holy and godly lives in view of the certain coming of the Lord Jesus.

READING OF 2 PETER 3

Prayer:

Lord, may I grow in the grace and knowledge of our Lord and Savior Jesus Christ. To Him be the glory, both now and to the day of eternity.

MEDITATION PASSAGE FOR TODAY:

verses 8–14, 18

This simple but profound epistle urges us to live out what we profess and to enjoy true fellowship with God by walking in His light, love, and life. It contains a perfect blend of truth and love, firmness and graciousness, exhortation and consolation, warning against false teaching and witness to what is genuine. This powerful little letter both encourages us and challenges us in our faith.

In his prologue, John remembers the apostolic fellowship with Christ and desires to share the joy of that fellowship with his readers (1:1–4). This fellowship is conditioned by walking in the light and is made possible by the blood of Jesus (1:5–10).

READING OF 1 JOHN 1

Prayer:

Lord, You are Light, and in You there is no darkness at all. When we walk in the Light as You Yourself are in the Light, we have fellowship with one another, and the blood of Jesus Your Son cleanses us from all sin.

MEDITATION PASSAGE FOR TODAY:

verses 1–3, 5, 7–9

C hrist is the believer's Advocate with the Father, and those who know Him must do what He commands—love one another (2:1–11). John wants his readers to grow into maturity in the word and to overcome the evil one (2:12–14). He cautions them against the lures of the world system (2:15–17) and against the false teachings of the antichrists who deny that Jesus is the Christ (2:18–27).

First John is not easy to outline because of the way it subtly interweaves and develops various themes such as light, love, life, truth, and righteousness. John makes use of several antithetical ideas in this epistle: light and darkness, love and hatred, truth and error, love of the world and love of God's will, righteousness and sin, the children of God and the children of the devil, the Spirit of God and the spirit of the antichrist, life and death. While this is a profound and multilayered epistle, John achieved this with a disarmingly simple vocabulary and style.

READING OF 1 JOHN 2

Prayer:

Lord, I know that when I sin, I have an Advocate with the Father, Jesus Christ the righteous; and He Himself is the propitiation for our sins; and not for ours only, but also for those of the whole world.

MEDITATION PASSAGE FOR TODAY:

verses 1–2, 15–17, 27–29

Not only must we abide in God's light; we must also abide in God's love (2:28–4:21). To do so is to enjoy God's assurance and to practice righteousness, since the practice of sin is incompatible with the believer's new nature (2:28–3:10). When believers sin, they do not reflect the regenerate new person, but the works of the devil. Regeneration produces righteousness, and righteousness is expressed in sacrificial love for others (3:11–24).

First John develops the theme of fellowship with God in belief and in practice and argues that belief in Jesus as the Christ becomes evident when it is expressed in actions of love and service of others. John sought to encourage his readers to obey God's command to "believe in the name of His Son Jesus Christ, and love one another, just as He commanded us" (3:23) so that they would enjoy the assurance of Christ's life in them.

READING OF 1 JOHN 3

Prayer:

Lord, I affirm the greatness of the love You have bestowed on us, that we would be called children of God; and such we are. We know that when Jesus appears, we will be like Him, because we will see Him just as He is.

MEDITATION PASSAGE FOR TODAY:

verses 1–3, 11, 16, 18–24

Those who have the Spirit of God not only acknowledge the incarnate Christ and the doctrine of the apostles (4:1–6), but also manifest the love of God in their relationships with other believers (4:7–21).

Because of its refutation of Gnosticism, 1 John stresses the incarnation of Jesus Christ: "every spirit that confesses that Jesus Christ has come in the flesh is from God; and every spirit that does not confess Jesus is not from God" (4:2–3). The one who denies that Jesus is the Christ denies both the Father and the Son (2:22). Jesus is the Christ who "came by water and blood" (5:6) — He was the same indivisible Person from His baptism to His crucifixion.

READING OF 1 JOHN 4

Prayer:

Lord, You manifested Your love for us when You sent Your only begotten Son into the world so that we might live through Him. In this is love, not that we loved You, but that You loved us and sent Your Son to be the propitiation for our sins.

MEDITATION PASSAGE FOR TODAY:

verses 4, 7–11, 15–18, 21

To trust in Jesus as the Christ is to abide in God's life and to enjoy the assurance of eternal life in Christ (5:1–13). "These things I have written to you who believe in the name of the Son of God, so that you may know that you have eternal life" (5:13). This assurance leads to confident access to God in prayer (5:14–17) and the power to overcome the evil one (5:18–21).

John emphasizes the need for belief in Jesus Christ (the Greek word translated "believe" involves personal trust and not merely intellectual assent), and says that this is the condition for the reception of eternal life (3:23; 5:10–13). Jesus Christ, the righteous One, is our Advocate before the Father, and "He Himself is the propitiation [satisfaction] for our sins; and not for ours only, but also for those of the whole world" (2:1–2).

READING OF 1 JOHN 5

Prayer:

Lord, You have given us eternal life, and this life is in Your Son. He who has the Son has the life; he who does not have the Son of God does not have the life.

MEDITATION PASSAGE FOR TODAY:

verses 1–6, 11–14

S econd John offers us a brief word of encouragement to continue to walk in God's light by loving and serving one another. It also warns us to be aware of spiritual counterfeits that distort the truth of the gospel of the incarnate Christ. Thus we are to love, but we are also to show discernment; truth without love leads to harshness and severity, while love without truth produces sloppy sentimentality (cf. "speaking the truth in love"; Ephesians 4:15).

John wrote to encourage his readers not only to hold firm to the apostolic doctrine and practice which "you have heard from the beginning, that you should walk in it" (v. 6), but also to warn them to avoid false teachers and not to take them in or welcome them. They must love one another in the truth and practice discernment so that they do not fall prey to deceptive influences.

READING OF 2 JOHN

Prayer:

Lord, may I walk in Your truth and obey Your commandment to love one another, just as Jesus has loved me.

MEDITATION PASSAGE FOR TODAY:

verses 3–6

The theme of this epistle is the importance of maintaining fellowship and undergirding the ministries of people who have committed their lives to sharing the message of new life in Christ. John wrote this brief letter to commend Gaius as a fellow worker in the truth because of his hospitality and support of missionaries who had been sent, evidently by John, to teach and equip believers in the churches in the region of Asia Minor. At the same time, this letter rebukes the pride and misconduct of Diotrephes in his rejection of those who teach the truth. John also commends Demetrius (who may have delivered this letter) to the church and informs Gaius of his plan to visit the church and settle the difficulties. The apostle starkly contrasts a man who wants others to look to him and another man who wants others to look to Jesus. One is the embodiment of selfishness and the other of servanthood.

READING OF 3 JOHN

Prayer:

Lord, may I walk in the truth and rejoice when I see others do the same. May I imitate what is good and avoid what is evil.

MEDITATION PASSAGE FOR TODAY:

verses 3–4, 11

J ude combines the style of his brother James and the theme of 2 Peter to create a brief but powerful word of warning and exhortation. Many of the New Testament epistles confront the problem of spiritual counterfeits, but Jude is the most passionate in its denunciation of their teachings and practices. This epistle serves as a potent reminder of the reality of the spiritual warfare that is all about us, and it teaches us that complacency leads to surrendered territory, while commitment to the Person and cause of Christ will keep us from stumbling.

Although his initial intention was to write "about our common salvation," Jude realized that in view of the growing threat of heretical teachers, he had to urge his readers to "contend earnestly for the faith which was once for all handed down to the saints." Thus, his primary purpose in writing this epistle was to expose the character and tactics of the ungodly deceivers who were infiltrating the churches and seducing believers to follow in their immoral path.

READING OF JUDE

Prayer:

Lord, to You who are able to keep me from stumbling, and to make me stand in the presence of Your glory blameless with great joy, to the only God my Savior, through Jesus Christ my Lord, be glory, majesty, dominion and authority, before all time and now and forever.

MEDITATION PASSAGE FOR TODAY:

verses 3–4, 20–21, 24–25

G enesis reaches back and portrays the beginning of all things, and Revelation reaches ahead and portrays the consummation of all things in God's judgment of humanity and creation of a new cosmos. This powerful Apocalypse (this word means "unveiling," "disclosure," "revelation") gives us a prophetic look at the completion of God's program and purposes for human history and elevates our minds and hearts to the sovereignty, majesty, wisdom, power, holiness, and dominion of the eternal Alpha and Omega.

The Revelation of Jesus Christ begins with a prologue (1:1–3), a salutation which portrays the triune God (1:4–8), and a theophany (a visible manifestation of God) of the omnipotent and omniscient Christ who will conquer and rule all things (1:9–20).

READING OF REVELATION 1

Prayer:

Lord, Your Son is the faithful witness, the firstborn of the dead, and the ruler of the kings of the earth. He loves us and released us from our sins by His blood – and He has made us to be a kingdom, priests to His God and Father – to Him be the glory and the dominion forever and ever.

MEDITATION PASSAGE FOR TODAY:

verses 4–9, 17–19

E ach of the messages to the seven churches in chapters 2–3 refers back to an aspect of John's vision of the resurrected Christ and contains a command, a commendation and/or condemnation, a correction, and a challenge. The seven messages are tailored to the specific needs of these churches, although some expositors have also seen in them a relevance that goes beyond the first-century context. Others see them as portraying some of the general movements in the history of the Christian church.

The rewards for the people of God who "overcome" include: eating of the tree of life; being unhurt by the second death; receiving a new name and the names of the Father and the Son; gaining the morning star; being clothed in white garments; and sitting with the Lord Jesus on His throne.

READING OF REVELATION 2

Prayer:

Lord, may I never leave my first love; when I am tempted to pursue lesser lovers, may I look to Jesus and return to Him.

MEDITATION PASSAGE FOR TODAY:

verses 7, 11, 17, 26–28

There are four primary approaches to the interpretation of the Apocalypse: (1) The *symbolic* or *idealist* view argues that this is not a prophetic book, but a symbolic portrait of the cosmic conflict of the spiritual forces of good and evil. (2) The *preterist* view (from the Latin word for "past") holds that Revelation symbolically refers to events that took place in the first century Roman Empire. (3) The *historicist* view interprets Revelation as an allegorical overview of the history of Christendom from its inception to the second advent. (4) The *futurist* view sees the first-century Roman persecution and emperor worship as a type of a far greater conflict that will take place in the future. According to this view, Revelation 6–19 portrays a coming seven-year tribulation that will be terminated by the second advent of Christ.

READING OF REVELATION 3

Prayer:

Lord, may I always respond to Your loving initiatives, and may I be zealous and repent when You reprove and discipline me for my good.

MEDITATION PASSAGE FOR TODAY:

verses 5, 12, 19–21

T he glorious scene in chapters 4–5 brings us into the presence of the triune God. The Father is worshiped as the holy and eternal Creator of all things (4:1–11). The Son is worshiped as the worthy Redeemer who purchased for God with His blood people from every tribe, tongue, people, and nation (5:1–10). The Father and the Son together are worshiped in 5:11–14.

Because of its highly symbolic nature, many who have read the Apocalypse have slipped into one extreme of concluding that it is inexplicable and therefore unfruitful to study, or the opposite extreme of speculating about every nuance in the book. It is more profitable to take a middle course: much of the symbolism of Revelation is explained in the book itself and in other books, such as Ezekiel and Daniel. However, there are a number of things that remain mysterious in Revelation, and we should not be overconfident in supposing that we can decode every part.

READING OF REVELATION 4

Prayer:

Lord, You are worthy to receive glory and honor and power; for You created all things, and because of Your will they existed, and were created.

MEDITATION PASSAGE FOR TODAY:

verses 1–5, 11

G enerally speaking, those who hold the symbolic, preterist, and historicist views are *amillennial* meaning Christ's kingdom is taking place now in a spiritual sense or *postmillennial* meaning Christ will return after the church establishes His kingdom by evangelizing society. Those who hold the futurist view are *premillennial*. Futurists believe there is a spiritual sense in which the kingdom has already come, but after His second advent, Christ will also establish a geopolitical kingdom that will last for a thousand years and will be followed by the creation of a new heaven and a new earth.

Thus, one's perception of the purpose for which John wrote the Revelation depends on which interpretive approach one takes. However, all would agree that one purpose of this book was to encourage its recipients in a time of persecution by assuring them of God's ultimate triumph over the forces of evil. It was also written to challenge them to persevere and to hold fast to the truth, because God will reward those who love His Son.

READING OF REVELATION 5

Prayer:

Lord, worthy is the Lamb who was slain to receive power and riches and wisdom and might and honor and glory and blessing.

MEDITATION PASSAGE FOR TODAY:

verses 5–6, 9, 12–14

Chapters 6–18 portray a time of earthly tribulation and heavenly conflict that centers around three cycles of seven judgments: seven seals (6:1–8:5), seven trumpets (8:6–11:1), and seven bowls (15:1–19:6). There are prophetic inserts between the sixth and seventh seal and trumpet judgments as well as a lengthy supplement between the trumpet and bowl judgments. In addition, chapters 17–18 describe the overthrow of "the great harlot" and of Babylon the Great.

After the three cycles of judgment and the wedding supper of the Lamb, the Lord Jesus Christ returns to the earth in power and glory to overthrow the beast and the kings of the earth (19). Jesus comes in majesty to reign over the earth as the King of kings and Lord of lords.

READING OF REVELATION 19

Prayer:

Lord, blessed are those who are invited to the marriage supper of the Lamb. He is the Word of God, the King of kings, and Lord of lords.

MEDITATION PASSAGE FOR TODAY:

verses 6–9, 11–16

I n this chapter, the Lord confines Satan and reigns on the earth for a "thousand years" (verses 2–6), defeats Satan and his forces in a final conflict, and judges the dead. Those who are a part of the first resurrection will not be touched by the second (spiritual) death, but those whose names are not written in the book of life will be judged at the great white throne and cast into the lake of fire.

Revelation blends apocalyptic, prophetic, and epistolary literature into a unique whole that uses ecstatic visions, admonitions, figurative language, graphic images of worldwide judgments, and sublime renderings of God's glorious character and reign. There are many parallels between the beginning in the first three chapters of Genesis and the new beginning in the last three chapters of Revelation.

READING OF REVELATION 20

Prayer:

Lord, I know that an hour is coming when the dead will hear the voice of the Son of God, and those who hear will live. For just as the Father has life in Himself, even so He gave to the Son to have life in Himself; and He gave Him authority to execute judgment, because He is the Son of Man.

MEDITATION PASSAGE FOR TODAY:

verses 4–6

A new heaven and earth is created, this time unspoiled by sin, death, pain, or sorrow. The New Jerusalem (described in 21:9–22:5), is shaped like a gigantic cube, fifteen hundred miles in length, width, and height (the most holy place in the Old Testament tabernacle and temple was also a perfect cube). Its multicolored stones will reflect the glory of God, and it will continually be filled with light. But the greatest thing of all is that believers will be in the presence of God, and "they will see His face" (22:4).

The Apocalypse has been given an appropriate place as the last book in the canon of Scripture because it ties the themes of the Bible together. In a very real sense, chapters 21–22 are the new Genesis, but without the fall. In broadest terms, the Bible conveys the metanarrative of God's work in creation, redemption, and re-creation, centering on the incarnation of the God-man.

READING OF REVELATION 21

Prayer:

Lord, in the new heaven and new earth, You will dwell among us, and we will be Your people. You will wipe away every tear from our eyes, and there will no longer be any death; there will no longer be any mourning, or crying, or pain; the first things will pass away.

MEDITATION PASSAGE FOR TODAY:

verses 1–7, 22–27

Revelation concludes with an epilogue that assures the readers that the Lord will come soon (22:6–21). Jesus Christ is portrayed in Revelation as the sovereign Ruler and Judge, and His might, majesty, power, and dominion are seen throughout this book. The titles ascribed to Him in the Apocalypse include: the faithful witness, the firstborn of the dead, the ruler of the kings of the earth (1:5); the first and the last (1:17); the living One (1:18); the Son of God (2:18); He who is holy, who is true, who has the key of David (3:7); the Amen, the faithful and true Witness, the Beginning of the creation of God (3:14); the Lion that is from the tribe of Judah, the Root of David (5:5); the Lamb (5:6.); Faithful and True (19:11); The Word of God (19:13); King of kings and Lord of lords (19:16); the Alpha and the Omega, the first and the last, the beginning and the end (22:13); the root and the descendant of David, the bright morning star (22:16); and the Lord Jesus (22:21).

READING OF REVELATION 22

Prayer:

Lord, Your Son is coming quickly, and His reward is with Him; He is the Alpha and the Omega, the first and the last, the beginning and the end. Come, Lord Jesus.

MEDITATION PASSAGE FOR TODAY:

verses 3–7, 12–13, 16–17, 20